Secular Parenting

In a

Religious World

Practical Advice For Free-Thinking Parents

Be-Asia McKerracher

Cover courtesy of AIVIA

Photo of the author courtesy of Elizabeth A. Bishop

ISBN-13: 978-1499309188

ISBN-10: 149930918X

For Rebecca, who reminded me that flying isn't

just for birds.

And for my family.

There's no better joy to me than to

be called mom and wife.

Contents

Secular Parenting
In a
Religious World

Introduction

In 1998, a young college student at the University of Wyoming, Matt Sheppard, was savagely beaten and murdered. When the late Pastor Fred Phelps[1] decided to picket Sheppard's funeral—specifically because he'd found out that Sheppard was gay—Phelps ushered in the smallest of his flock to do his bidding. America watched as the tiniest of tots were seen holding signs and wearing shirts that read "God Hates Fags" and "No Fags in Heaven". I was barely 18 at the time, without children, and with no real connection to what was happening to Sheppard's grieving family. I also had no

---

[1] Of the Westboro Baptist Church

idea how those small children, holding the most degrading of signs, would be forever changed by the choices of their parents.

Five years later, the gravity of both Sheppard's death and the role of children in religion collided when I was assigned a book called Losing Matt Sheppard[2] by my English professor. And while the book more than adequately outlined the death of Matt Sheppard, as well as challenged our assumptions of gay and lesbian people in America, it was my class conversations about the role of children in organized religion that left the strongest impression. The picketing of Sheppard's funeral by the Phelps children showed how overzealous adults, on a mission, can shape and control the minds of small children.

The Phelps family isn't alone in their use of children to spread a religious message. In 2006, the documentary Jesus Camp allowed Americans to peer into a popular Christian summer camp for Evangelical children. The nation watched—in a bizarre mix of horror and curiosity—as the larger than life youth pastor, Becky Fischer, told of a world where we (Americans) should teach our children to give up their life for Christ the same way that young Muslims are taught to give up their lives in Madrasas for Allah[3]. Fischer actually says "children are so usable" as she boasts about her

---

[2] By Beth Loffreda

[3] According to Fischer

ability to walk onto a playground and "have children speaking in tongues" in a matter of minutes.

The behavior of the Westboro Baptist Church and Becky Fischer paint a dim picture of faith and young children. I should be clear, these examples do not constitute the totality of a child's experience with faith. They do show how easily faith can be manipulated for nefarious purposes—and how quickly children can become unsuspecting victims.

All religious doctrines do place a high value on children. The Bible, for example, tells us to "raise up a child in the way he should go, and when he is old he will not depart from it." Likewise, the Quran reminds us that "every child is born with a true faith." [4] Directives such as these leave little room for doubt in the mind of most parents: children, according to most faiths, need faith.

But do they?

In the last 20 years the number of parents choosing to raise "faithless" children proves this idea false. Secular parents have created a border between their child and the tenets of faith. This "mental fence" against organized religion is necessary for several reasons. Most importantly, young children lack the basic reasoning skills to analyze the questions that religion poses; children need time to develop their critical thinking skills. How else will they be able to evaluate religious claims as they mature? As parents we must look

---

[4] The assumption being, of course, that the true faith is Islam.

out for more than just their physical safety. We must also focus on how our child's mind is altered by religious doctrine.

So instead of creating a fence that bars our young people from exploring the mysteries that lie at the heart of all religions, our fence needs to be a fluid one that allows young people to discover faith on their terms—at their pace—with parents as their most valuable guide. From this perspective, a child can be raised without faith **and** have the character traits that create a well-rounded adult: compassion, self-discipline, an understanding of right and wrong, and a real sense of their value in this world.

That is the "spirit" embodied in this book. *Secular Parenting in a Religious World* is a guide to help parents explore faith with their children. They need knowledge to make good choices, and that includes the knowledge embedded in religious texts. How your child discovers that knowledge requires serious consideration.

Keeping our children's minds open to *all* of life's possibilities means that we keep them grounded in what is right, while at the same time allowing them to explore. We can do that as parents by keeping our minds open to possibilities, learning all we can, and transmitting those truths to our youngsters with as little bias as possible.

-Be-Asia McKerracher

1

To America, With Love

This book began with a lie. She was three years old when she told it, and I owe my daughter so much for her poor attempt at deception. I was standing at the kitchen window watching my girls play in the backyard. When I saw my oldest daughter hit her sister, I called her in for a talk. To my disappointment, she lied point-blank to me. Not a moment before, I had seen her smack her sister, yet she lied to my face. In those early days of my parenting experience, all I could think was, I'm honest with her, so why isn't she honest with me?

I needed a set of values to help guide my daughters' thoughts and actions. Initially, my only focus was punishment. I didn't want my girls to lie to me again. Though my husband and I had decided to attempt secular parenting, I thought that maybe my daughters did need a bit of religion—if only so they would be afraid enough to do the right thing in the future! That was how I was raised: with the idea that some kind of all-seeing capital-G "God" can see you if you're bad. Even if no knows, God does. But fear did not necessarily prevent me from making bad choices as a child, and I knew that it wouldn't keep my daughters from doing the same.

As such, my daughter's lie is essentially the reason I wrote this book. I want to address the need to raise critically-thinking, moral children motivated not by religious fear but by parental love and their own powers of reason.

I think it's fitting that before we begin our journey together, we take a moment to clear up any misconceptions that might be floating in the back of your mind. I want to make it clear that *Secular Parenting in a Religious World* is not intended to be an all-inclusive manual for raising a child. No book can be. The goal is to offer a guide for the many parents across America who wish to raise children to be freethinking individuals. Current Pew Research Polls have indicated that in the last ten years, a sharp change in the relationship between Americans and faith has taken place. No doubt that has left some families in a sort of limbo: Do we raise our children the way we were raised or do we chart new parental territory?

If you're reading this book, you may be leaning toward the latter. You are not alone. Almost twenty-five percent of Americans polled on the subject of faith identified themselves as "religiously unaffiliated." This poses two main questions:

How can millions of people across America bestow upon their children a respect for the faithful while simultaneously teaching them to think critically about religion?

How can we teach religion to young children without indoctrinating religious dogma? In a society struggling with conflicting religion and secularism, too few books address these concerns.

Personally, our family has experienced both the ups and downs of the secular parenting journey. My husband and I are dedicated to teaching our children the truth no matter how hard it is to accept, a principle you as a parent no doubt share. We hope that you learn from both our successes and our mistakes.

Because this book is not all-inclusive, I have made every effort to fill it with useful, factual information that you are welcome to verify, including books, websites, and other information that may be of interest to you in your efforts to educate and raise your little darlings. A large part of secular parenting—and secular life in general—will involve your willingness to search for the most accurate information with which to live your life and guide your child-rearing practices.

Secular Parenting in a Religious World is also not an assault on religion. You won't find an atheist screaming for religion's head in this book. Religion is a philosophy that guides the lives of many Americans, and I have neither the time nor inclination to seek its eradication. However, I do believe that it is crucial that it be both investigated and studied. All philosophies—if not explored, turned inside out, and rethought—can breed ignorance. We must be willing to investigate the philosophies that guide our lives if we are to continuously grow, and we must teach our children to do the same.

I have little doubt that the very religious may find some of my views objectionable at least, blasphemous at worst. Please note that faith, like all else in our society, is subject to inquiry. All that I have done here is question those religious practices and ideas that may be a detriment to raising tolerant, critical-thinking children.

My goal is for both secular and religious parents to read this book. We live in a time where war and difference makes us afraid. We fear those who don't look like us, think like us—pray like us. With all the differences that exist in the world, the only way to give our children a fighting chance in any society is to teach those skills that are universal: self-awareness, merit-based judgment, empathy, and, most importantly, critical thinking.

The Mini-Me Phenomenon

Through our children comes a new generation of opportunity and hope, the power to teach about the beauties and complexities of life, and the joy and innocence that we rarely see in such a chaotic, mean world. We see all this and more in the faces and hearts of our children. Yet for all that we see, there remains a profound blind spot in our vision: We fail to comprehend our children's uniqueness as individuals with all the rights therein.

But what does this mean? Surely we acknowledge that children are individuals. In courts of law, they have the right to choose which parent with whom they want to live. Furthermore, children are afforded protection *from* abusive parents and others who would do them harm. These aspects we easily recognize because they are physical. But children are not just physical individuals; they are mentally unique as well. Are children then allowed to marry at age ten if they "feel ready"? Of course not. Classifying children as individuals consists of recognizing their ability to think and respond differently from us, their parents, while still guiding them toward adulthood. We allow this in society on every level except faith. Why?

On the surface, most parents know this to be true. Of course our children are unique individuals. Again, everyone tends to agree until religion enters the mix. If I were to say, "Of course our children are unique individuals, but just because we the parents have chosen to be Christians, Muslims, or atheists does not mean that our children need make that same choice," most parents would respond less certainly.

The truth is that children *are* unique in *all* aspects of their lives, including their religious affiliation. The trouble is that, through centuries of tradition and ritual, this freedom gets lost. Since most parents will agree that children are individuals with their own likes and dislikes, why exclude their like or dislike of religion? What makes a child bound to the religion of their parents?

In my research for this book, many adults told me that they wished their parents had given them the chance to choose. One Catholic professor cited her lack of choice as a child as the reason she never wanted to have children of her own. Sadly, many parents have laid out their whole child's life as soon as the child is conceived: he will attend private school; she will most certainly take piano lessons; he will go to college; she will marry a doctor or lawyer.

Does this book suggest then that we as parents should not actively help our children pursue their future? What about cultivating the emotion and beauty that comes with the spiritual aspects of life?[5]

---

[5] We'll talk more about spirituality near the end of the book. For now, I consider spirituality as a part of the human experience separate from religion.

Is that out of the question as well? *No.* We can hope, of course, but ultimately the future belongs to our children.

In the end, what we as parents *don't* see in our children is what is most crucial: We don't see their right to truly exist independently from us. By taking the time to step back from our (non)faith, we can begin to teach children those universal understandings that are present in all (non)faiths. We can show young people that our love for them stems from a desire to see them at their best in life, even if *their* version of best doesn't coincide with ours.

This starts with truly identifying our children as belonging to themselves. Our role as parents then becomes rather diverse. In their early years, we are nurturers and safety providers. At the elementary level we become role models and "explorers-in-chief". During the teen years, we grow into guidance counselors. By adulthood, our children hopefully see their parents as bearers of wisdom.

Secular parenting allows us to adapt our understanding of children's individual needs at specific stages of their developing life in a realistic and pragmatic way. We do this with the knowledge that our ultimate aim, our ultimate desire as parents, is to create happy, healthy, productive members of society and citizens of humanity.

Why Let Children Choose?

The very young in our society lack a level of critical thinking that would help them *really* understand what religion is and if they agree with religion's worldview. Until they mature, it is important that we separate morality and faith. This is especially true for the very young child in three important ways. First, children between the ages of two and seven have a difficult time focusing on more than one aspect of a situation. Typically, the most immediate receives the most attention. For example, what if a child were asked the following question: "Don't you want to go to heaven and be with Jesus and see Grandma when you die?" Children do not consider the possibility that Jesus or heaven could actually *not* exist. All the child knows is that Grandma once did exist, she's not here anymore, and seeing her again would be nice.

Children in this age group also have difficulty tracing the steps in a situation back to its original source. Of course, my goal is to help you change that. I want inquisitive young people in America, children who aren't afraid to keep thrashing through false logic until they arrive at their own conclusions. Imagine a child being told that Noah could only take two of each animal on the ark. The conversation might go something like this:

Parent: So Noah loaded up the ark, two of every kind, and that's how he saved all the animals.

Child: Why did Noah leave the other animals to die?

Parent: Because that's what God wanted.

Child: What about the babies? Did God not want them?

Parent: Of course he did. God is love and God was saving the animals from the flood.

Child: Why did he make it rain so much? If there was no rain, all the animals would be OK.

Parent: Remember the beginning of the story? Those people were bad.

Child: Were the animals bad too?

It might sound like an annoyance, but that is *exactly* the type of child we should all want! A questioning child is a thinking child, and whether the subject is religion or why we have to eat vegetables, questioning is something that we should encourage. Instead of looking at the moral of the story (God had to kill all the bad people and, sadly, the animals as well), this child couldn't get past the fact that God actually left behind those he loved. Why did he do that? The more we can get young people to look beneath the surface issue and dive into the logic of a situation, the better their critical thinking skills will be.

Finally, between ages two and seven, children tend to focus on things as they first present themselves. This is particularly difficult when trying to separate fact from tradition in many faiths. If, for instance, children are told that Mohammad flew to heaven on a winged horse—and that image is cemented in their minds as truth—it becomes horribly difficult to be objective about such an assertion. By this stance, a child is as likely to believe that Hogwarts School of Magic *really* exists or that Gandalf's staff *actually* stops Sauron's evil. Without presenting what faith teaches in the context of what we know to be true (in this instance, that there are no winged horses), we deprive children of their ability to think rationally as they age.

I'm sure someone out there will holler that a child's imagination is sacred and if we raise them "logically" they'll be about as much fun as Spock. There are thousands of secular parents in America and around the world who put logic at the forefront of their child's life experiences. Those same children still play dress up. They still put on fake capes and fly around the house. They are still children. The difference is that they have a stronger ability to beat back those illogical precepts that can infect a young mind.

When you think about these three traits (listed below), one can see the signature of our nature: These traits are survival skills. Our children have the luxury of being at the top of the food chain, but if one were to switch a human child with any other animal that uses basic instincts to survive, a clear pattern emerges.

They focus on one aspect of a situation at a time. Primarily, they focus only on what their parents do since the parents keep them alive.

They focus on the here and now (or risk maiming and death).

There is no time for second guessing. In the wild, a second guess can cost one's life. The parents are always right. No matter how silly or irrational it seems, *the parents are always right.*

In his fiery book, *The God Delusion,* Richard Dawkins also acknowledges this trait of young people. He says,

We survive by the accumulated experience of previous generations, and that experience needs to be passed on to children for their protection and well-being . . . There will be a selective advantage to child brains that possess the rule of thumb: believe, without question, whatever your grownups tell you. (174)

How sad it is that religion meets our children before they have the full control of a mature mind, and how important it is for us as parents to be aware of this unintended reality. Running on basic instincts makes it impossible for a child's mind to logically interpret and analyze the viewpoints religion proposes.

At that point, a child isn't choosing religion; they are being indoctrinated to believe in the basic tenets of a particular faith. It's an ugly truth, and we need to change that. Indoctrinating a child is like taking advantage of a person who is mentally ill and as such cannot think for him or herself. By *indoctrinating* I do not mean *teaching*. We teach our children the things that will help them to be successful in life, from not hitting to chewing with one's mouth closed.

I am speaking of the indoctrination that alters a child's ability to rationally view a situation: to instruct in a doctrine, principle, or ideology in a biased way. I see no reason to expect a child to make an informed decision on the issue of whether or not God is real. Why should they be asked to decide whether or not one religion is the "true" religion until they reach an age where they can logically judge what makes sense? Modern religions

- refuse to acknowledge and deal logically with the facts that children will need to survive in what has become a fragmented society;
- promote a high level of intolerance for others; and
- provide children with an answer to many of life's questions that defies logic and is unquestionable at the same time.

I don't mean that religion maliciously corrupts the young. We as parents have a responsibility to guide our child through the web of faith; otherwise, the results skew toward a close-minded child. We see this time and again in society. The detriment that religion can cause to a child's developing worldview—intolerance, scorn, and ignorance of known facts—does not justify any of the benefits religion supposes to offer. Love, community, investigations of the afterlife, and moral and ethical guidance can be found in other places while your child grows into adulthood. As secular parents, we must teach our children that religion is one option of many that attempt to understand the world, and they alone must decide which religion is best for them. Take, for example, this true scenario that occurred at my daughter's elementary school her first grade year.[6]

Setting: An elementary school cafeteria at lunchtime. Essence, a first grader, has her lunch tray and is walking toward her classroom's table. Brianna, her best friend, has saved her a seat.

Brianna: I saved you a seat here, Essie.

Essence: OK.

Essence sits down and begins eating and talking about gym class.

Kale: Essence, Michael said that you told him you don't believe in God.

Essence: *(Breathing deeply)*. I don't. My mom said that God isn't real.

Silence.

Kale: You're going to hell!

---

[6]We should keep in mind the fact that I wasn't present during the encounter; this is what happened according to my daughter. I also changed the names to protect the identity of the children.

Essence: My mom said that hell isn't real either.

Kale: Yes, it is. That's where you go if you don't believe Jesus died for you.

Essence: I do believe in Jesus. My mom said he was a probably a real person who lived a long time ago, but he only died for himself.

Classmate: My mom says you're bad if you don't love God.

Brianna: Essence, you are bad if you don't love God. He's waiting in heaven.

Silence.   Essence stares at Brianna.

Essence: I'm not bad. I never hit people or bully people. I'm not bad because I don't believe in God.

Brianna: Well, I guess I do know a girl who's badder than you, and she does believe in God, but she's still bad.

The conversation continued to trail on in the same vein. From their religious beliefs, these children learned two devastating lessons:

1. Complete intolerance for people who think differently from them: if you're not in our group, you're not a good person; we hate you.
2. Physical suffering is OK if people don't belong to your group: If you won't join our group, you will burn in hell; we hate you.

To be fair, these were not bad children or children of Christian fundamentalists. Having volunteered in my daughter's class and worked with all of the children there, I can tell you they were average American kids who went to church about once a week—and they thought my daughter was evil because she did not believe in their God. They did not consider her kindness, her lack of bad behavior, or the fact that they had spent every weekday for the past year with her. She was evil because their parents and their church told them so.

Since almost all children tend to parrot their parents (even Essence took the familiar "my mom said" as a fallback), secular parenting provides a more open-minded attitude for young children to emulate until they *do* begin using independent critical thinking skills. This is something as parents we should *all* cultivate in our children.

Sadly, the situation with Essence happened because of a child's understanding of the Christian faith. To a young child, it's all or nothing: You're either with us or against us. It is not until they mature that they realize the world isn't so black and white. That is why children must be fed religious doctrine cautiously and with plenty of discussion. Fast forward twenty years. Children raised to be intolerant and separatist are now adults who rule the world. Will they work toward the peaceful coexistence of *all* of humanity? Will they still show contempt for those who are different? Will they use their power to suppress those ideas which contradict their upbringing? Multiply these few children by all the religious beliefs in the world today. You now have billions of individuals who are programmed not to work together but to do their part for their particular group. How will humanity function cooperatively?

That's why we must open our children's minds to all religious viewpoints in a nonbiased way. A child should learn about the various points of view religions offer under the objectivity of parents, family, and friends until they are old enough to decide which ideology they want to take in life. A child should be cultivated in reason, logic, and critical thinking. These are the skills they need to survive the onslaught of evils that man can bestow upon man. Religion should be viewed as one of the *many* ways to look at life's big mysteries rather than the emphatic "only."

Your child deserves the option of openly questioning religious texts and beliefs because they are individuals like you and I. *We* question every choice we make in life. Shouldn't they? In this way, religion becomes a way for your child to better understand the origins of life and the mysteries of death on their own terms. Religion ceases to be the divisive, intolerant machine that it has unfortunately become when children are allowed to rationally choose.

Centuries of religion have stunted parenting skills as well. Much-needed conversations about sex, morality, and relationships are replaced with phrases like "sex before marriage is a sin," "x, y, and z will result in eternal damnation," etc. Today's youth get no practical advice for dealing with real-world situations because we as parents foolishly refuse to believe such situations can occur.

Because of the fear tactics religion uses, we as parents often avoid necessary but difficult conversations about condom-use, addictive drugs, and much more. Young adults are left with stone-wall rules that don't hold up at the basement parties, the sleepovers where boys get access, the playgrounds when no teacher is near. I am working hard to raise smart, healthy children without the aid of religion—and most of you reading this are either doing the same or strongly considering it.

Our children are not perfect. I personally have no doubt that they will make mistakes—they are children and that is how children grow in wisdom—but I have faith that the mistakes they make will not be life-threatening. I have prepared my own children for a world where both decent and cruel people live. I invite you to keep reading and do the same. My children are grounded in reality and their critical thinking skills will continue to develop as my husband and I instill a value of intellectual honesty, self-reflection, change, and respect for others in a diverse society. This book is for the secular parent, the religious parent, and all the parents in between. Take from it what you may. My hope is that, together, a community of freethinking parents and children of *all* kinds will emerge.

2

E.T. Phone Home:
Are Children Innately Drawn to Their Heavenly Home?

It's been a long-held belief that children are innately closer to God than adults could ever be; their pure hearts and immature minds somehow leave them open to God's divine purposes. To separate a child from this type of spiritual pureness is considered by many as wholly immoral. There are certainly passages in every religious text that say to bring a child "steadfastly up in the faith." But *are* children innately closer to God? No surprise that I argue *no* here. If we are really going to give children back to themselves, there can't be any strings attached.

Children are no closer to God than anybody else. By claiming that they are, we strip children of their right to investigate religions with an open eye and a critical mind; we teach them to see every faith but theirs in a hostile, close-minded way. There are, however, many who would disagree. The only real way to find the truth here is to analyze the logic that says children are innately connected to God in order to figure out if the logic makes sense. While an entire book could be written that refutes these claims, I'm going to stick with a couple of popular ones by Sofia Cavalletti and Tobin Hart. Both of these books make similar claims on the divinity of your children while ignoring the faulty logic that they are built on.

In Sofia Cavalletti's book, *The Religious Potential of the Child*, she offers three qualities that bring children closer to God:

1.   Children innately are drawn to the Lord.
2.   Children have mysterious knowledge.
3.   Children can see the invisible.

The back cover of her book reads, "[This] is not a "how-to" book, complete with lesson plans and material ideas. Instead it offers a glimpse into the religious life of the atrium, a specially prepared place for children to live out their silent request: 'Help me be closer to God by myself.'"

Tobin Hart's book, *The Secret Spiritual World of Children* makes a similar claim. The subtitle of Hart's book reads, "The breakthrough discovery that profoundly alters our conventional view of children's mystical experiences." If we are to give our young people the freedom of choice they need, we must first divorce the idea of "the child as divine." Our children deserve to be looked at objectively as individuals, not vessels of our desires (or God's, for that matter).

I should note that while *The Religious Potential of the Child* focuses on the Catholic tradition and *The Secret Spiritual World of Children* focuses on the Christian Bible's New Testament, all major religions have a set of guidelines for children and their religious instruction (oddly enough, none offer children a choice in faith). Though different faiths will certainly have different rituals, the claims on a child's innate divinity have been widely been accepted as true. Let's examine the underlying glue that holds each claim together.

Claim #1: Children are innately drawn to God.

According to this claim, children have a bond with God that will shine through, even if the child has no formal religious instruction.

Many people believe God works through children and that to fail to raise your children with God's word is to deprive them of their divine right, but I maintain that this is false. Its true goal is to spread faith before children can think for themselves. If a child appears to possess an unusually strong closeness to faith—for whatever reason—they are used as a model for childhood divinity by the ardently faithful. But if we exclude religious texts as an objective source of truth on this matter, what *actual* proof is there that young children are divine? Cavalletti's book offers a dozen or so examples of children who came to God on their own accord. Take Lorenzo here:

Who would believe that a four-year old child would be capable of metaphysical intuition? Lorenzo belonged to a Catholic family, but he had never had any [religious] instruction, nor had he received any special care in the religious sense. One day his aunt asks him to do a picture of God. Lorenzo drew on the bottom left-hand side of the page—and hence in a secondary position—a human figure with a large head, and then he filled the page with a series of signs in which numbers could be recognized. His aunt asked him the reason for the presence of the numbers, and Lorenzo explained: because there are many." Lorenzo had the intuition that God is infinite. (32)

OK, so little Lorenzo's drawing probably looked like this:

To be fair, I'm one of those super-proud parents—don't we all have a bit of this parental pride in us? Young Lorenzo here was asked to draw a picture of God and his response was a drawing similar to the one above and the sentence "There are many." His aunt—who was no doubt a strongly religious woman—saw Lorenzo's actions as proof of his connection with God. This is a pretty weak connection logic-wise. It certainly isn't enough to qualify a child as being divinely inspired.

Another child in Cavalletti's book, Charlotte, was drawn to the Lord through an innate connection that no parent fostered.

Charlotte (three and a half years old) was staying at her aunt's house. When she saw her aunt preparing to leave, she asked her where she was going; the aunt replied that she was going to Mass and the child declared: "I am coming too!" And so it continued for days, without the slightest urging on anyone's part.

One day another child came to play with Charlotte and she told her aunt that she would not be going to Mass with her. Then a moment later she was back again saying, "Stefano can wait. First I'm coming with you!" (37).

Again, there are so many factors that need analyzing here. Never mind the fact that some children, like my youngest daughter, would live in a car if it meant they could get out of the house and run around town. Other children, like my oldest girl, think a trip to the store is about as exciting as watching paint dry. Cavalletti, and those who unfortunately fall victim to this type of logic, fail to realize the varying spectrum of reasons why a child does anything. To narrow the focus to "child and God" leaves out the most important, and probably the most significant, connection: the relationship between caregiver and child. When my sister-in-law Sarah is in town, my girls would go anywhere with her. They love her so much, and because they rarely get to see her they would happily exchange playing outside for going on trip with their aunt.

Let me be clear here: I'm not attacking Cavalletti personally. That is unnecessary and pointless. I want us to look critically at the claim itself, and there's plenty to critically evaluate in both these scenarios that promote the divinity of a child. For example:

Why was Lorenzo not asked to explain how the sentence "There are many" relates to God? He could look at the numbers on the picture and explain that he put a lot of numbers on the picture. We just don't know.

The logic behind Charlotte's story is all wrong. The logic says, If Charlotte's aunt is going to Mass and Charlotte wants to go, then Charlotte has a divine connection. That's like saying, if I'm going to Midas and my child wants to come, then my child must have a special connection with mufflers and brake pads.

How do numbers, randomly placed on a child's drawing, show God's infiniteness? Could the child just have been doodling despite the aunt's directive to draw God?

Who says Charlotte isn't just an outgoing girl who relishes getting out of the country and going to the city?

I could go on, but my point should be clear. There are so many variables at play. Pinpointing a child's divinity based on a random picture or clingy disposition is ridiculous and devoid of critical thought.

Tobin Hart's interpretation of children being innately spiritual is also full of logical holes. In his book, *The Secret Spiritual World of Children*, Hart describes his daughter's "chat" with the late Mahalia Jackson, an American gospel singer. While working on a report for class at the age of nine, Haley came across many "unique" facts about Ms. Jackson in her research. When her father questioned her, she proceeded to tell [him] a wide range of very subtle and personal information about Mahalia Jackson that [Hart] could not find in the materials she had read—[he] checked (21).

When Hart asked his nine-year old how she came across the information, she said it was easy; I just got relaxed on my bed and asked my angel for help. Then, in my mind, I went to www.mahaliajackson.com, and there she was standing right in front of me. We talked and she told me about her life (21-22).

This is clear evidence, according to Hart, that "children [are] open to these depths of consciousness naturally and regularly." The problem here for Hart, and many others who hold to this claim, is the notion of clear evidence. There are serious questions about the validity of Haley's statement that should shoot into one's mind. The book doesn't say, for example, what materials the child already had access to, what specific statements were made, and whether or not Mahalia's close friends and family members could validate those statements. To believe anyone with facts as weak as this requires a tremendous leap *over* common sense.

Again, my goal here isn't to make a mockery of Hart or Cavalletti. I simply want to challenge their claim of childhood divinity. There isn't enough evidence to say childhood divinity is a valid label to smack on any child.

Claim #2: Children have mysterious knowledge.

According to this claim, children have the ability to know things before an adult explains it to them. This proves that they are divinely connected to God.

The claim that children hold mysterious knowledge is based on a child's ability to know the answer to a question that you didn't expect them to know. Cavalletti's example is as follows:

Many years ago I was presenting Baptism to a group of children from four to six years of age, and I was unsure whether or not to speak of the meaning of the imposition of the hands, thinking that it was too difficult for children of that age to understand. But in any event, I wanted to try. I put a ring in my hand and two or three times I extended my arm, opened my hand, and let the ring fall out, explaining that this is what I would do if I wanted to give them a gift. Then I repeated the gesture without the ring, saying, "At Baptism, the priest makes this gesture over the child; but you do not see anything fall. Then why does he do it?" The children replied in chorus, as if the question was completely superfluous: "Because he is giving us the Holy Spirit." (42-3)

First, the children's response in this situation rings of memorization at least, indoctrination at worst. The fact that they knew what his hand gesture meant isn't mysterious. Children will amaze you with the things they pick up about the world. As parents, we've all seen it at least once. They learn these facts (or, in many cases, false information) from school, playdates with friends, logical deduction, and good old-fashioned guesswork. Take my youngest, for example. She tends to be a bit messy. One night at dinner, she was pouring milk into a glass when we heard a loud *splash!* When I went into the kitchen, she had the milk container in her hand, her glass was broken in two, and milk was streaming down the cabinet. She didn't know how the glass broke. She said, "I took the glass out of the dishwasher, poured the milk in, and the glass broke."

Aha! I'm not a science whiz, but when I felt the glass it was piping hot. "Do you know why the glass broke?" I asked her. I was all prepared to talk about heat and cold and how mixing them too quickly can make the glass break. My daughter stared at the glass for a minute and said, "Oh, so when the cold milk mixed with the hot glass, the glass couldn't figure out if it wanted to be hot or cold, so it broke, right?"

I was shocked. It wasn't the most scientific answer, but it basically described what I was going to say to her. Now, I didn't *expect* her to know that; she logically deduced why the glass broke, and she happened to have been right. (I also didn't sign her up for science camp that summer.)

The point is, yes, at times children can display extraordinary understanding in an area where we didn't explicitly teach them. This is a wonderful consequence of good parenting and exposure to the world. With your guidance, children will hone and develop this skill as they mature. Your praise and encouragement after an unexpected answer will give them the confidence to try new things. Such instances will *not* prove, however, that they are innately divine.

Claim #3: Children can see invisible beings.

This claim says that it is a fact that children can see invisible things, almost as if it were more tangible and real than the immediate reality.

This is by far the most fantastical claim made by people about the divinity of young children—and it drives me crazy. I remember as a young child being told that I could see God like no adult had. If I only searched my soul hard enough, I would see him and he would see me too. Tobin Hart makes the claim that children can see the invisible in his book. He first acknowledges that in our daily lives, we are encouraged to believe something only after we see it for ourselves. . . . [We must] suspend our critical thinking . . . This does not mean abandoning our critical mind or being a naïve convert to some idea or doctrine; rather, it means turning off our critical judgment for a moment in order to open up to possibility. (116)

What's most depressing about his statement is the idea of turning off critical judgment to become open-minded. Critical judgment is a major factor in knowing the difference between open-mindedness and absolute stupidity. If we want our children to make good choices as they mature, they must know the difference between something that is *plausible* and someone trying to take advantage of them; their critical judgment is their only survival tool in such a situation.

So Hart gives us a young girl named Llael to expand his thoughts on the claim that children can see the invisible. Llael has three invisible guides that giver her support and protection in life. One is a wolf that protects her. Another is a Native American man who instructs her in the art of healing. The third is a spirit whose job is to help Llael gather all the children of the world together in harmony. Hart is a psychologist, and he describes Llael as a "psychologically healthy and well-adjusted girl" (119). He cites the "quality of her as a person and the quality of her answers" that lend credibility to her guides.

I think that as parents, we should take issue with Hart here for a couple reasons. First, the psychological well-being of a person should have no bearing on the reality of things that cannot be seen. I'm a psychologically healthy woman and right now and I'm looking at an eleven-foot tall pink rabbit. He has blue polka dots and a red ribbon around his neck. This rabbit, Gunter, helps me realize and display love and affection to my family. Gunter is not real, though. I made him up while sitting in this coffee shop and staring out the window. Psychologically healthy people can see things that aren't real too. It just takes a bit of creativity and imagination.

This leads me to another unfortunate fact that parents need to look out for when dealing with these claims of divinity: People are more willing to accept invisible beings that are good and do good deeds, but tend to dismiss invisible beings that cause harm or do negative things. We tell children that the boogie monster isn't real because he is bad, but persist in filling our children with the "reality" of the tooth fairy, Santa, and other "nice" invisible people. Psychologists are quite willing to tell a schizophrenic to dismiss the invisible beings and voices that can cause them to do harm, but in the same breath they will tell pretty twelve-year old girls with "guides" that they believe them completely. In truth, if people can see imaginary beings, then they can see *all* the imaginary beings equally. Goodness shouldn't be a determining factor in whether or not they exist.

This chapter may make me sound like a monster, and that's OK. There are dozens of books that make this claim on young children: a claim of divinity. I maintain that we as parents give young people the right to choose, as free individuals of society, the philosophy that will guide their lives. We cannot do this if we allow others to place a brand of God on their existence before they learn the many religious philosophies that exist in the world.

In the end, the three reasons for the divinity of young children don't hold up. Children are not divine beings. They are individuals trying to grow and learn, to find their place in this world through trial and error. Our job as parents is to support them in this endeavor and give them the skills they need to explore the world in a safe and healthy way. Separating children from religion is not separating them from a divine right. Any interaction a child has with religion needs to be closely monitored for understanding and should only be done when a child has the critical thinking skills to evaluate the religious claims being made.

What's in a Name? Redefining Spirituality

In October of 2013 Oprah Winfrey spent some time with long-distance swimmer Diana Nyad in an interview that quickly morphed into a discussion about atheism and spirituality. The then 64-year old Nyad spoke of an underlying sense of spirituality that she felt—though she maintained her atheism. Oprah retorted "well then I don't call you an atheist… "I think if you believe in the awe and the wonder and the mystery, then that is what God is. That is what God is. It's not a bearded guy in the sky."

But I would challenge Oprah's logic here. This awe and depth of emotion that connects a person to inexplicable feelings--whether in children or adults--is not some innate call to God. Children can express a level of spirituality without demonstrating innate religiosity. I find the word "spirituality" quite deceptive. We have turned the word into a blanket term covering anything having to do with relationships that exist outside the realm of proof, a connection with things unexplainable. I think some re-labeling is in order here. This is touchy territory because, yes, I am an atheist and, no, I do not believe in angels, devils, or other such beings. All the logic in the world cannot explain every connection that we as humans have: connections to family, birthplace, planet, etc. Consider the following experience I had not too long ago:

While sitting at my computer, a thunderstorm warning for my city flashed on the screen. Naturally, I got up from computer and went outside. Even now, as I see it so vividly in my mind's eye, my feelings are hard to explain. As I stood on my porch, I felt a slight wind tickle my arms. The sky was phenomenal. I looked up and the clouds seemed so close. They were gigantic gray-white swirls set on a yellow background with pink highlights in between. There was something that kept me watching those clouds. They were moving incredibly slowly and my eyes leisurely traced their path. I wanted to move, wanted to go back inside—I felt drops of rain—but I couldn't take my eyes off those clouds. I just stood there, looking deep into the white swirls. I was in total submission to those clouds. The rain—even the cool breeze—didn't keep me from watching them. I was connecting with them in a way that was so meaningful, so purposeful. I stood there for almost ten minutes with my eyes pointed to the sky and another five with my face pressed to the screen door, watching.

In the Midwest, opportunities like this present themselves on cool spring mornings, late evenings in the fall, and even in the dark of winter. I have pulled to the side of the road to revel in the beauty of a skyline and, when I do, I feel part of something magnificent. It would be nice to find a word that pointed directly to what I felt, yet only the word "spirituality" can fill such a void. But spirituality is a loaded and misguided word. It assumes that its root, *spirit*, is at the forefront of my thoughts. The reality is that my experiences have nothing to do with a spirit and everything to do with a sense of connection. How does one explain that to a child?

Try as they may, reason and logic simply cannot explain *everything* in the human experience. We are in the midst of creating a world where it is not considered religious to ponder the existence of other worlds, life-forms, and unexplainable feelings. As a society, we should instill in our children a sense of awe in the world around us—we should feed their natural curiosity about death or life on other planets. We should feed a child's natural curiosity for nature. It was curiosity and awe that inspired Galileo to study the stars, Thomas Paine to identify the rights of man, and W.E.B. Dubois to experience the human condition in America's South.

I can't be sure of what I felt that day, looking up at the sky. Words couldn't encapsulate my state of mind at the time. My feelings were beautiful and sacred, inexpressible. They were not, however, the hand of God, Allah, or any other religious figure. Those feelings were my own.

Secularists all over the world have similar experiences when they kiss their sleeping children, look into their spouses' adoring eyes, feel the grass on their bare toes in the early morning. The problem with defining what I felt—what you might feel on occasion—is that it is open to harsh scrutiny and misinterpretation. We must rename our experiences: I did not have a connection with God when I looked into those clouds in the pouring rain; I felt a connection with our world, a connection with the living things that reside on our planet, and the feeling left me moved and at peace.

Your child experiences many feelings in a typical day. I encourage you to slow their world down, take them outdoors, and show them that we really are part of it, of this world. I told my daughter that some feelings you simply cannot put into words. When your child discusses those feelings of deep happiness, sadness, or confusion that cannot be put into words, I encourage you to discuss with them the greatness of the human experience. It's not always possible to categorize one's feelings. Secular parents should recognize and accept this. Making our children aware of this reality will strengthen their curiosity and feed their desire to understand the world around them.

3

Morality Minus Faith: How to Raise Moral Children without Religion

If we acknowledge that children are individuals—and I hope by now that you do—then it goes without saying that children have the right to choose their religion and the guiding principles they will use to travel through life. Until they are of proper mental age to make such a choice, they should not be coerced by the rules of convention, tradition, or any other notions that slap a label on them.

The only way to give your child a moral foundation without religious faith is to peruse the pages of history. As I began to question what it meant to be moral, I found myself in the philosophy section of the library many a night. I came across the writings of Robert Ingersoll, or "The Great Agnostic," as he was called. In the twenty-first century it is easy to speak of secular living since a growing segment of the American population ascribe to such a lifestyle. In the late 1800s, however, to do so could put one's life in jeopardy. Despite this, Ingersoll gave sweeping lectures across the country advocating a closer look at religion, which ruled the lives of most at the time. He gave a now-famous lecture entitled "What would you substitute for the Bible as a moral guide?" His goal was to open the conversation of morality beyond the scope of the Bible. (My hope is that you take some time to skim it.)

While Ingersoll noted that the New Testament had a few moral guidelines he considered worthy of following, many important things are left out: "You would have nothing of human rights," he wrote, "nothing in favor of the family, nothing for education, nothing for investigation, for thought and reason." He ended the statement by saying, "It may be that no book contains better passages than the New Testament, but certainly no book contains worse."

While we have been traditionally taught that the source of our morality is divine in nature, Ingersoll, like this book, advocated a better approach. As parents, I believe we should be concerned with two things:

- Do we as parents have a working understanding of what it means to be moral?
- How can we teach our definition of morality to our children?

The dictionary definition of morality is "beliefs about what right behavior is and what wrong behavior is." Essentially, morality is the product of our experiences from childhood to present. We learn to make moral decisions from our own parents, our friends and family, and our community or society at large. With this attitude, it's no wonder young people are developing poor reasoning. For example, in some parts of America, it is socially acceptable to make racist comments or tell racist jokes. Parents and other family members do it and children mimic it. In doing so, they incorporate those ideas into their moral code.

As we mature into adolescence, our morality is challenged not only by society but by uncontrollable hormones and irresponsible peers. Ideally, our teen years prepare us to make independent moral decisions and we become seasoned adults with strong moral grounds. The key word here is "ideally." We may not be able to give a fancy definition, but most of us instinctively know when the choices that we make are right or wrong. Translating that feeling into a concrete set of values can be difficult, especially when trying to convey those values to young and immature minds. It involves constant awareness of our words and our actions as parents.

For example, if we see homeless people in our community and we teach our children to not stand near or talk to them, then we have instilled in our child a moral that says, "It's OK to be insensitive to the needs of those less fortunate than you." But if we have our children visit local homeless shelters and pass out food or clothing, then we have taught our children to help those less fortunate in a safe and satisfying way.

Defining Morality for Young Children

We as secular parents must address morality with our little freethinkers openly and honestly. As I described in the first chapter, when my daughter turned three I realized that she could (and did) willfully lie to me. What I came to understand is that all people— children included—choose to be moral or immoral based on the information they have. Ingersoll knew this, and I think, deep down, we all do. Yes, we are given warnings by those that love and care for us: don't do this, *do* do that. But in the end it is our own will that prompts us to make choices of right and wrong.

The word *morality* is slippery and used in many ways. We must first define morality as best we can and what it means for a child to be moral before we can provide experiences and knowledge that enhance a child's moral reasoning.

Most of the definitions of morality involve how a person behaves in public, a person's character and will, and the expression of truths that one person conveys to another. We all know these rules and most parents teach them dutifully to their children: don't steal, don't lie, don't hurt others, receive permission to touch others' things, and—our personal biggie—treat people the way you want to be treated. But, again, we find ourselves as parents telling our children what to do. The goal is to have children think for themselves, so we must come up with a different approach.

Trying to explain morality to young children is cumbersome. They do not have the wisdom to see that not everything is black and white and that each decision must be judged on its own merit. Take the following situation for example. I came across a study when I was trying to figure out how to teach morality to our girls. It was presented to children ages ten, thirteen, and sixteen by Lawrence Kohlberg, an American psychologist. While many philosophers speak of morality, Kohlberg specifically sought to figure out what children thought morality meant, how they rationalized morality, and what we could learn from that knowledge. Read the small narrative that Kohlberg read to children:

In Europe, a woman was near death from a special kind of cancer. There was one drug that the doctors thought might save her. It was a form of radium that a druggist in the same town had recently discovered. The drug was expensive to make, but the druggist was charging ten times what the drug cost him to make. He paid $200 for the radium and charged $2,000 for a small dose of the drug. The sick woman's husband Heinz went to everyone he knew to borrow the money, but he could only get together about $1,000 which is half of what it cost. He told the druggist that his wife was dying and asked him to sell it cheaper or let him pay later. But the druggist said: "No, I discovered the drug and I'm going to make money from it." So

Heinz got desperate and broke into the man's store to steal the drug for his wife. Should the husband have done that?[7]

Kohlberg's point wasn't whether or not your child would answer yes or no (though if you tell them about Heinz and his dilemma, I bet you'll get some interesting answers). Kohlberg wanted to learn why a child thought it was right or wrong to do something. After much research, he concluded that children pass through moral stages of reasoning which can vary from child to child. What's more, a close look at Kohlberg's findings reveal that children are guided by instincts when it comes to morality in the same way that they are guided by instincts when it comes to listening to and following their parents' lead. Essentially, children are programmed by years of evolutionary trial and error to follow their parents' guidance as a survival tactic.

The first stage of Kohlberg's moral reasoning—the pre-conventional level—occurs in a child's early years. It essentially states what we already know: young children follow the rules and guidelines of their authority figures. This is no secret to us as parents, but it is a very real asset.

---

[7]Initially Kohlberg's study was only conducted with middle- and lower class boys. He then expanded his research to include girls, younger children, and children from various parts of the country and the world.

For you and I, this translates into many opportunities to show children our moral character. For example, one of our family morals is donating to those less fortunate. We donate gently used clothes, toys, and other household items whenever possible. By _we,_ I mean that our children play an active role in donating with my husband and myself. They come with us to donating stations, they hand the items to the people, and they say "you're welcome" when thanked for the donation. We teach them that it is our obligation to help others in our community any way we can. As they age, they can participate in charity walks, Arbor Day tree plantings, and other community events.

As a child moves into the second level of Kohlberg's moral reasoning—the conventional level—children begin to consider the thoughts and feelings of others in greater proportions. This coincides with children going into school and learning to listen and pay attention to the feelings of classmates, teachers, other students, and those in the community at large.

The wonderful thing about stage two is that it also coincides with a rapidly growing understanding of the world. Children during this time gain incredible amounts of knowledge through school, home, and community about people, culture, and how the world works. This is the best time to teach the commonalities in the human experience, the value of differences, and the idea of critically looking at situations, people, and ideas. As thoughtful parents, instilling the moral necessity of kindness, diversity, and love—all varieties of life—

will enhance your child's natural love of and respect for others. By the time children reaches the end of the second level of Kohlberg's reasoning, they see the rules of society as the basis for morality. Those rules are followed without question. Kohlberg believed that most adults remain at this level of moral reasoning.

But Aren't the Rules of Society Always Changing?

Fifty years ago, homosexuality was synonymous with insanity. One hundred years ago, miscegenation—or interracial marriage—was punishable by incarceration. And today, in our advertisement-driven society, anything attached to a half-naked woman is desirable. Are these the morals that we want for our children?

Kohlberg answers this question in the final stage of reasoning, the post-conventional level. It is something that very few people achieve, according to Kohlberg. He estimated that only about twenty-five percent of adults achieve the post-conventional level of moral reasoning. Here, a person realizes that the laws created by society are just that: laws that reflect society's current—and often transient—views. These views can be altered based on the will of those who live in the society. Ingersoll, with his outspoken views on the relationship between religion and morality, was definitely at this stage of moral development. The key, of course, is getting your children to a place where they can understand that a *legal* rule can be wrong if it violates their standards for what it means to be *moral*. Then the challenge is to have young people objectively look at their "moral rules" and challenge their own moral logic to see if their reasoning stands strong.

After reading Kohlberg, I realized that the only way to raise a child's moral reasoning was to realize that children need experiences that flex their moral muscle. I cannot tell my daughter to be kind to her classmates—I'm not in her classroom and I can't see if she's doing that. She must make the decision to be kind in the absence of her parents. The same is true for your children. They must have the character and sense of self-respect to do the right thing when they are away from their parents. Morality, then, can be taught without explaining intricate levels and stages to young children—or even memorizing it yourself. Morality can be simply defined as *making the best choice in a situation when no one can see you.*

Was it the best choice for Heinz to steal the medicine when no one was looking? My oldest daughter, who was seven when I quizzed her, said yes. She acknowledged that stealing was wrong. She also felt sad that this man was losing his wife to cancer. If there was a treatment, the woman should have it. She thought it was unfair for the man to sell something for such a high price when poorer people needed it. She called him greedy and said he could have had lots of extra money if he'd taken the $1,000 because $1,000 is much bigger than $200. She thought the druggist should be the one who goes to jail.

Part of me was pleased with her answer. After looking at both sides of the situation, she made the decision she thought best. Had she been a bit older, we could have discussed how laws are made, how companies make money, and how to keep poor people from being exploited by those same companies.

How your child answers is not as important as the logic behind their choice. This logic can tell you a wealth of information about their moral muscle. Did they consider *both* sides of the situation, both the druggist *and* the husband? Did they think about what would happen to Heinz if he stole or what should happen to people who sell things at ridiculous prices?

I told our children outright that it's incredibly difficult to do the right thing when no one is looking! To help our children decide what would be the right thing and why, we play the "What if?" game. I ask them, "What if you were alone in your classroom and there was lots of candy on your teacher's desk? Would you take any?" Children are smart; most kids will say no. So play the devil's advocate: "You mean to tell me that if no one was looking and you wouldn't get into trouble, you wouldn't take one small piece? Wow. That's hard to do." Along with this we add a thinking question: If you're only a good person when people are looking, if you only make good choices because you are afraid of people seeing you do bad things, are you really a good person inside?

The answer to this question is no. It is harsh, but there is no reason to beat around the bush here. If you are only good because you fear getting caught, going to hell, or some other such penalty, than you are not being good for the sake of being good—and you should do some self-evaluation. You are being good because you are afraid of punishment. Fear will *never* breed a productive, critically thinking member of society.

We must make our children aware of the fact that they can choose to do the best thing in a situation—specifically, the thing that will not hurt anyone or themselves. Stealing candy from a teacher's desk is wrong whether or not you get caught because you have hurt your teacher by taking her things without permission; you have made her afraid to leave you alone with her things because you will not respect that ownership. You have hurt yourself because people will stop trusting you if you cannot respect their property.

The truth sounds good, right? Unfortunately, very young children look at morality and rules as one thing. If a child is punished in a negative way for hitting her brother, then hitting is wrong and should not be done. It is not until a child is older that they learn, yes, in some instances, hitting is the best and right choice, such as if you are being repeatedly hit by a bully or if someone is trying to kidnap you. In the latter case, hitting may save your life.

In one sense, mixing rules and morality is a good thing. We make rules so that people do not hurt others or themselves and so everyone in our community is respected. In another sense, mixing rules and morality can be very dangerous. Like Kohlberg's example, we need young people to consider the many options that can be made—as well as their ramifications—before a decision can be made. Take, for example, the racist laws enacted to keep blacks and whites from marrying. Was that a useful, good law? Back when black people were thought of as property, that answer might be yes. But we have grown as a country, seen the error of our ways, and, consequently, the error of the laws that kept that way of life working. Children should learn that a rule that unnecessarily stops a person from doing something they want—even though they are not hurting anyone or themselves—is not the best rule.

The Walls Have Ears

Just as your rules will dictate how your child behaves morally, your thoughts and ideas on a given subject will also shape their sense of what is right and wrong. This is where we as parents must be extra careful to show our children that there are many views on a given subject. We must question our own beliefs and allow our children to do the same if they are ever to make good choices of their own. For example, those unconscious stereotypes we may hold, those things that we hold so dear, deserve to be presented to children objectively. When my aunt would holler that "the Republicans were . . ." or that "Gays were asking a lot these days . . ." she told me how to morally respond to each of these groups of people. Take the issue of gay marriage, for example. If we tell our children that two men or women marrying *is* wrong, then we have etched the following into their morality schema:

- People who marry the same sex are not good people.
- We do not like people who do wrong (and therefore morally bad) things.
- If you want to marry a person who is a girl or a boy like you then you are not a good person and I will not like you because you will be bad.

We must be careful on any subject in which there is an opinion-based answer to *not* state our opinion as fact. Whether we agree with homosexuality is not the point. Your child will live in a world where some people find homosexuality repulsive and others see it as the only way of life for them. To give your child both the facts of a situation and your own moral stance, and then to reiterate that they will have to make the decision for themselves as adults, is the best way to enhance your child's moral reasoning. Let's say we change the sentences about homosexuality to the series of statements below:

- Some people choose to marry the same sex.

- Many people are upset about that because *they* believe it is wrong.

- Some people also think it is OK.

- I personally believe [explain personal beliefs], but when you get older, you can decide who *you* want to marry.

- No matter who you choose, I will love you.

What you have now done is given your child an objective view of the subject, your moral opinion *and* the opinions of those around them. They will take all that into consideration and as they reach adulthood, they will make a decision. They will *not* hate homosexuals, commit atrocities against same-sex couples, or enact laws or devise customs that openly show unwarranted aggression toward homosexuals.

There are, of course, fact-based statements that can be turned into opinions. A pedophile can say, "It is my opinion that children are sexual beings and they enjoy sex with adults like myself who love them back." The facts of the matter are that, yes, children can have sexual responses to stimuli. Baby boys have erections, some children enjoy touching their private areas, and by the time children are over age seven they are naturally curious about bodies. None of these facts suggest that children understand the ramifications of pregnancy, sexually transmitted infections, the function and purpose of sex, the emotions surrounding sex or insertion (and the definite pain that would come from such an act at their age). We outlaw pedophilia because only half the people involved in the act of sex can truly call themselves "consenting."

In the end, if you really want your child to have a working knowledge of what morality means and to grow in moral wisdom, it is important to

- be open and honest about life in general (No, babies don't come from storks.),

- enhance their critical thinking about moral situations by giving them opportunities to decide what they would do in a situation and discuss their response,

- create a non-biased home (as much as any human can, because no matter what some biases will be present) so that children can *really* think about a subject without feeling guilty, and

- instill a sense of empathy for other people and their possessions and a desire to treat others the way we want to be treated. It is particularly crucial that we as parents live that reality so our children can see it enacted in everyday life.

Caution: The Pious Deserve Respect Too

A large part of morality is the idea of respect, so it is with a personal plea that I add respect for the pious to the end of this chapter. We may not realize it, but we secular parents are quite cynical. We hone in on logic and we forget that that trait, while great, can come at a cost—namely, disdain for the overly religious. I have fallen victim to negative comments born out of sheer frustration many a time and, I can tell you, my girls swallowed that animosity whole. Even as we learn to hold our tongues as adults, children do not always get the memo.

One day, my daughter and I were at the store waiting in line to pay for groceries. As we were talking, I let out a sneeze and the woman behind me said "God bless you." I smiled at her and said, "Thank you." My daughter looked at me like I'd committed a crime. She began to comment, "We don't believe . . ." I stopped her and tried to save the moment with an awkward smile. When we got in the car and she began talking about what had happened, I told her that God was not a bad word. It is my hope that if you are a secular parent, you always keep in mind that God is not a bad, evil, or taboo word. It is a word that describes a concept in which many people find comfort. Let me replay our conversation for you.

Essence: Mom, why did you say "thank you" to that woman who said that God was blessing you?

Me: Well, a long time ago, people used to believe that when you sneezed, your soul—the part that is supposed to go to heaven if you believe in God—

came out of you. To save your soul, people would say "God bless you."

Essence: Do you believe in a soul?

Me: No, but today we mostly say "bless you" or "God bless you" when you sneeze because of habit. Even though I don't believe in God, it would be rude and mean of me to yell at her because she wanted to do something nice.

As the days went on, I pointed out to my girls the difference between being courteous and trying to make someone believe in something. This was a hard thing for them to understand, and it may be hard for your child to understand as well, but it is incredibly important. One thing children must learn about religion is that not everyone is convincing them to believe in God if they say the word "God." The reason younger children tend to have trouble with this is because they are still looking at the world in a "black or white" sense. Either you're religious or you're not. Either you believe in God (and have permission to use and accept the use of religious words and phrases) or you don't (and aren't allowed to use or receive any religious words or phrases).

It will take lots of discussion and lots of time for them to reject this false dichotomy. It may not even happen until they are much older, but it is very much worth the time you'll put into it. To help our girls begin to move from a black and white sense of the world to a more holistic understanding, we began pointing out religious concepts and ideas that overlap in our society. Here are a few examples.

1.   Not all music with the words "Heaven" or "God" is bad.

Now, I am clear with daughter about my views. I listen to the song because I like how it makes me feel, but I don't believe in Sinead's God or that heaven is real. I also tell her that it's perfectly OK to like a song that has the word God or heaven in it. Those are not bad words. My daughters also really like that Sinead's God is a woman.

2.   If someone is trying to do something nice for you and they believe in God (and use God's name), you don't have to dive into a religious conversation.

It is common for secular parents to take *every* mention of God or religion as an opportunity for a lengthy discussion on the subject. <u>This is not necessary and can backfire on your ultimate goal of creating a free-thinking child!</u> If your ultimate goal is to create productive citizens who can decide for themselves whether or not to follow a certain religion, leave them alone and let them choose.

I've made my understanding of the world known to my children, as I'm sure you will make yours. So I leave them alone. When they ask me a question, or when I think real understanding on a subject needs to be made, then I open a discussion on the subject. But if someone says "God bless you" to them, or if someone thanks the Lord for something in their presence, I keep my mouth closed for a couple of reasons. 1) The person was trying to be nice. I want my children to understand that people express kindness in different ways. As long as it doesn't infringe on their right to think and believe how they want, it doesn't hurt. 2) Children need to see that people do these things and that it is a choice that they really do have.

It's not easy, and you might find yourself fidgeting because you itch to say something, but keep your mouth closed unless asked! Give your child's mind a chance to make connections and learn about the society in which they live. They will thank you when they are older.

3. Do not fear conversation about religion around family or friends.

Now this can be tricky if you haven't already came out of the secular closet. We will talk about this in detail later. The important thing to remember here is that you have the right to think and feel the way you do. There is no reason that you or your child should feel bad about the secular path that you have chosen. People who love you will respect that.

Caution: At family events, you and certain family members may engage in a game of "who can have the last influence." Fun at first, this game can become a huge family spoiler. To avoid feeling like I was losing influence, or that my children were being unduly subjected to religion, I simply had a short conversation with my daughters before family came to visit. It sounded something like this:

"Grandma and Grandpa are going to spend the week with us. Grandma and Grandpa believe in God, heaven, and hell. I just want you to know that you can choose to believe in those things if you want to. You also don't have to talk about religion if you don't want to. You can tell Grandma and Grandpa that you don't want to talk about that right now, and that you want to talk about something else. If someone is making you feel uncomfortable or bad about that, you can talk to me or Dad about it, OK?"

This type of conversation helps children prepare for what might be unexpected, and I do it every time we enter a situation that we don't typically encounter, such as praying at meals or ceremonies such as marriages that involve religion. It doesn't involve coercion; it simply prepares kids for something foreign, and I answer any questions they have as objectively as possible.

I'm sure if you thought about it, you could find places and situations where the topic of God or religion would come up in your daily travels with your child. Those are the best opportunities for exposing your children to groups of individuals who think differently than you. Remember that our job is not to create little versions of ourselves. Our job is to create productive members of society. To do that, your child must interact with those who are different from you in a safe and controlled way. As their parent, you will know which situations present such opportunities.

In the end, no child is perfect, and many adults find it difficult to make the right decision in a given situation. For better or worse, many aspects of morality are fluid (though, no, killing a person is never OK). But deciding, for example, whether or not a person's actions should qualify them for the death penalty has evolved many times. Being an empathetic parent will surely allow your child the security they need to grow morally. Take the time to explore your child's mistakes in judgment, and then be sure to congratulate them on their moral successes. Soon, this reflective aspect will become a part of your child's natural way of thinking (and yours as well). None of these moral realities, however, demand a religious faith at the head of the conversation.

4

Foundations of Success: Self-image, Self-worth, and Critical Thinking

The purpose of this chapter is to focus on the little things that we do in parenting, those daily rote exercises that, without our knowledge, actually shape who our young people will become. Like any parent, when people comment to me that my girls are "so well-behaved" or "just so respectful," I beam with pride. The secret to cementing any idea in a child is consistency. Christianity says to "train a child up in the Lord so that they will not falter." I say, train a child up in common sense and decency, and they will prosper. There's no way that I'd ever grow or learn as a teacher if I was never given professional development. Likewise with our little tykes, training must be offered on a consistent basis to ensure a wise citizen of humanity.

No need, however, to break out the parenting manuals for this one. Laying a foundation for success is simple if you can follow this one rule: consistency. I so enjoyed writing this chapter because it took me back to the early days of being a mom: the dirty, smelly, crying, down-in-the-trenches days filled with the same phrases repeated dozens of times. Priceless, right?

Right. I doubt my children would be who they are today without the time and effort put into creating and sustaining a routine that included affirmation and unconditional love. If you're reading this book, then you are all too aware of this fact and are working in your home on these things as well. I maintain that a secular parent—every parent for that matter—uses affirmation and love as a way to shape and mold strong future citizens.

The first step to creating a child that can live productively in any diverse society is to foster a positive sense of self-dignity and -worth. This is more crucial for a secular child because, as we have already confirmed earlier, their self-image and self-worth will be under constant attack to conform to religious norms. Raising children that can defend themselves mentally—against adults as well as children— will rid them of much frustration later in life. It will also teach them to stand firm on their principles. Here are some tried and true tips that I think we can remind ourselves of:

Allow your child to make choices about as many things as possible.

A quick story is an order here. On my daughter's first day of school, she beamed with pride. Instead of wearing the cute plaid skirt I'd bought for her—complete with Mary Janes and stockings—she had designed her own kindergarten outfit: thick flannel, multi-colored stockings, shorts (that didn't match the stockings), a striped shirt, and tennis shoes. Her smile was ear-to-ear. She grabbed her backpack and stood firmly at the door, ready for her new adventure! I, on the other hand, stood speechless. Was I really going to let her leave my house looking like a bizarre clown? She wasn't matching. She was wearing red *and* pink. I wanted her to change. Before I said anything, my husband came around the corner and said, "You look great! Let's go, everybody."

My husband's response was worlds better than mine. If you take a look at any child-rearing book, you will find that children who are given choices about their surroundings tend to be more willing to allow others those same rights. The terrible twos (which really don't have to be terrible) are all about a child's need to affect their surroundings as the sole controller. Giving up control—or allowing children to feel empowered—can be difficult. The deciding factor in the amount of control most parents give their children boils down to the amount of control they had as a child. There seems to be a natural law that follows parenting: Unless we make an effort to learn more, we generally tend to parent the way we were parented. Take a glance at the following table. Can you find your parents, or yourself, in it?

If you were raised in a(n) . . .	you are more likely to . . .
authoritarian home where there is little choice and many rules (too much structure)	raise your children the same way *or* create an environment with few rules.
free-flowing home where there are few rules (too little structure)	raise your children the same way *or* revert to a strongly structured home.
balanced home with both rules and choice (right amount of structure)	raise your children with the same balanced approach.

This is a rudimentary chart, a bare-bones perspective about how family structure can control the way you parent. But we have so many resources out there for learning what works, for trying to figure out how to help your child maneuver in the world that we need not limit in the same way limited (or failed to limit) ours. I do not fault my mother for her parenting. What was she supposed to do but what she thought best? We, however, live in the age of technology; we have no excuse for not searching out the best ways to parent, trying new things, and learning through failure.

Once aware, you can change your parenting habits to allow choices in your children's lives that help them feel responsible. For children to grow into thoughtful adults, they must have practice making decisions about how they will live their lives from an early age. The only way to get the confidence and self-esteem necessary to make difficult decisions and redirect behavior is through practice. You'd be surprised at how much choice your children can have. In a typical day in my home, our children choose their

- breakfast
- clothing
- hairstyles
- homework times (though once chosen, this tends to stay set)
- seats at dinner (and the menu for one dinner per week)
- bedtime stories
- tooth-brushing length (two or three minutes)

Finally, they get to choose whether or not to give hugs and kisses to us before bed. Now, my children cannot choose whether or not they brush their teeth, stay up past their bedtime, or eat whatever they want; good parenting requires some rules that cannot be choices. The good news is that a child can have rules *and* freedom of choice at the very same time. I encourage you to let your children take pride in their ability to care for themselves—especially if you don't always agree with their choices. Allow them to feel that they do have control over their environment. As long as what they choose does not endanger them, or break the rules and routines you've set up in your home, every choice will create a lesson that will pay off in your child's future.

Eventually, structured choices emerge. For example, yes, I let my daughter go to school looking like Punky Brewster for most of her early years. She'd go to the store looking like our family had no real sense of matching colors and patterns. It was so hard. I would say things like, "Are you sure that's what you want to wear?" Her reply was always a definite "yes."

Once she entered the fourth grade, though, we began talking about the "solids" and "busies." I told her to choose a busy and a solid. Two busies are less attractive. So she began to choose black pants with that wild shirt or a plain pink shirt with her busy skirt. And, yes, by middle school, she wanted to wear what everyone else was wearing—*but* she always kept her own sense of style. She wasn't afraid to be her own fashion self—and that, parents of the world, is the goal. We want children who aren't afraid to think differently from their peers.

Create positive self-esteem and self-worth.

I'm not writing this to insult your intelligence. Scores of books have been written about self-esteem and children. All children benefit from good self-esteem. The reason I add this to the list for secular children is twofold. First because it's a good idea for everyone to feel good about themselves. But second, and more importantly, non-religious people—and that includes their non-religious children—are the most disliked people in country.

Have some doubts? Well, as late as June of 2012, at the height of frenzy over the republican presidential nominee Mitt Romney's Mormon faith, Jeffery Jones compiled a series of Gallup Polls on presidential candidates, faith, and public opinion. Atheists ranked far below many groups considered disenfranchised in America: blacks, Hispanics, women, and gay and lesbian individuals. The polling suggests that American's are *far* less willing to vote for an Atheist as the leader of the free world.

This dislike does not simply extend to presidential politics. Austin Cline, a well-known advocate for atheism and agnosticism blames the continued loathing of atheists on age old myths about people who don't believe in God. Generalizations such as *atheists are communists, atheists worship Satan, and atheists are immoral, selfish people* continue to corrupt the thoughts of so many. Why? Well, that's another book. Mostly it revolves around the actual questioning of a belief that is so intertwined with who people are that they become incredibly offended at the thought of purposefully rejecting God. Having had my daughter told that she's going to hell by a group of classmates, having to defend her right to be a freethinker, I can tell you the *only* thing that saved her from real mental damage was her firm belief that she was a good person, that those words weren't true, and that defending her position of "learner not preacher" was her right.

The best defense against negative self-worth is practicing responses to attacks on your child's self-worth. We call our practice sessions "What if" scenarios. The idea is to role-play situations that you know your child is sure to encounter. This gives them a fun way to deal with real-world problems that secular children face as they leave the safety of home. They are also fun, stimulating, and contagious. In our family, we sit in the living room and I say, "Let's play the 'What if?' game. Are you ready?" As they got older, the game aspect drifted and became a session for thoughtful questions. Here are some of my favorites:

1. What would you do if you saw a person walking down the street and a twenty dollar bill fell out of his or her back pocket?

2. What would you do if an adult told you that you had to believe in a God?

3. What would you do if your teacher said something that you knew was wrong?

4. What would you do if someone said they didn't like you because you had brown (or white or tan) skin? What would

you do if someone didn't like you because your hair was a different color?

5.   What would you do if someone told you that when you die you're going to hell? (Of course, that one comes after explaining and talking.)

6.   What is the difference between tattling and telling?

7.   What would you do if you saw someone bullying another kid at school?

This last question is particularly important. Kids should never sit by and allow another person to be mistreated. It takes bravery, but you can instill in your child a sense of duty to help those who cannot help themselves. Barbara Coloroso wrote a wonderful book called *The Bully, the Bullied, and the Bystander* designed for this purpose.

For younger kids, the "What if?" game is a way to explore who they are without eroding their self-esteem. For example, "Yes, your skin is tan. No, there's nothing wrong with that." For older children, writing these reminders on the refrigerator, posting them on the bathroom door, or just asking them is a great way to keep the lines of communication open. Think of situations your child or young adult is likely to be put in and abstract a question out of it. If a party's coming up, you might ask, "If there is alcohol there, will you feel pressure to try some? What would you do if you needed help getting home after having alcohol even though you knew it was a bad choice?" This may open up a conversation that you didn't expect, but if your children answer, it means it was on their minds as well!

Create a sense of unconditional love in your home. I'm not a quote junkie, but here is a quote that speaks directly to the question of what unconditional love is *not*: "My brother and I had different fathers, and, boy, did his dad let me know it." The person I took this quote from was the elder of two children. The mother remarried and the father of her youngest child made his love *very* conditional. When she was perfect, she was liked—but never loved. Anything less than perfection—which with kids, of course, is often—and she was despised by her stepfather.

Psychologically, we treat our children differently in subtle ways. After all, they are not all the same person. As responsible adults, it is our job to see to it that our children know—regardless of how they act, what kind of grades they bring home, who their friends are, what their concept of spirituality is, how they dress or any other quirk of their personality—that they are loved *unconditionally*. The easiest way to accomplish this is to make it a point to do something every day, no matter the day's events, to let your children know they are loved. Most parents choose a hug or a kiss at the end of the day, before school, or at some other specific point in the day. I've even seen creative parents stick letters in lunch boxes, on the front door, or on kitchen table. I try to send random text messages to my thirteen-year-old that say things like "I love you! Have an awesome day!"

Whatever you do, the last thing your child should question is how important they are to you. My children know that they are special to me because I say those exact words to them as often as possible. A parent should never assume a child knows this. Your children should be told how much you care about them—often!

Emphasize empathy. Every childcare center, elementary school classroom, and general place of social interaction has the basic principal to "treat others the way you want to be treated"[8] somewhere in its social contract. Yet many people fail to recognize the beauty and simplicity of its meaning. This is key to developing empathy in your freethinking child. A child must be able to see how what they are doing affects others; they must be made to recognize this above all else. Compassion for others also should extend to those who do not share your child's lifestyle, beliefs, or general outlook on life. The phrase "treat others the way that you want to be treated" should be posted somewhere so children can constantly be reminded that if you don't want it done to you, don't do it to someone else. When discussing issues of faith, I am careful to remind the girls to judge the tenets of the faith itself, not the people who choose to

---

[8]Many will argue that Christianity created this "golden rule." A close study of religious and cultural practices that predate Jesus, however, will show this same standard of human interaction. Buddhism and Taoism are good examples.

follow it. But this isn't limited to faith. The idea of treating people the way you'd like to be treated includes our most sensitive areas of society: what we do with the elderly, how we treat disabled individuals, and the sensitivity involved when discussing America's overweight population.

This is another case where exposing your child to religion—under the façade that it is completely true—can have damaging results. The world's major religions—Islam, Judaism, and Christianity—all defy our basic notions of empathy. How? They teach that if you are not one of them, then you are bad. This is not an overt message. No faith openly says, "Hey, let's hate everyone but us." But faith is an exclusive club with serious rules and consequences for not joining. It may be simplistic, but our children do not think in complicated analogies and metaphors like our ancient texts. How can we not expect children to go out into the world and show contempt for others when they hear parents, preachers, and loved ones speaking ill of people because of what they are not? Even if we were all American Christians, or American Muslims, would it be OK to degrade those that do not follow our chosen path? We may interpret the Bible, the Quran and other holy texts in any way we please, but what they teach in their texts (and thereby condone) is the cruel treatment of those who are not in your group or do not follow your God's prescribed rules for life. In the home of a secular child, there is no confusion—we treat people the way we want to be treated. Period.

But this is much easier said than done. For example, I don't spank my children, mostly because I don't want to be hit when I do something wrong. My motto is that people who love you don't (physically) hurt you. I believe that when our children arrive in this world, the last thing we as parents think about is spanking them. We want to help them make good choices as they grow. Spanking is the result of frustration and anger.[9] Even as a child, I thought it utterly meaningless when my mother would insist on a hug after spanking me. I would think to myself, *how can you love me when you forced me on the bed and whipped me until I could barely breathe?* What lesson was I supposed to learn from that? People who love you don't hurt you.

Foster stability. This is not negotiable. Every child, if they are to succeed in life, needs a home life that is stable, secure, and can provide for their basic needs. If you need help in areas such as financial stability, partner or spousal communication, abuse, drugs and alcohol, etc., you must get help before you can focus (with any degree of success) on creating an environment that will help your children grow to be the brilliant critical thinkers they are. Sure, you

---

[9] Only in the rarest of occasions can I condone spanking a child. Say what you like, but I believe there is almost always another choice.

can *provide* for children under these circumstances, but would you want to be raised under these conditions?[10]

I say this knowing that there are all types of families. But the type of family is not as important as the sense of security and trust a child's environment offers. All types of families can be stable: grandparent-led families, same-sex families, single parent families, and every type in between. Stability involves being able to count on the same things happening each day. As long as children have that, I believe they can leave the home and venture with confidence into the world.

Let's review those five strategies for enhancing self-worth and self-image:

- Creating **opportunities for choice** in your child's life.
- Creating **positive self-esteem** through questions, self-reflections, and affirmation.
- Making sure your child is aware of your **unconditional love**.

---

[10]And if you were, that is certainly no excuse to repeat history.

- Instilling a firm sense of **empathy** for others—regardless of their differences.

- Making sure your child has a **stable home life** that allows for exploration.

The order of these qualities is not important. Your child will venture out into a world that is filled with love, violence, beauty, contempt, and host of other benevolent and malignant situations. If we are to give them the respect of being an individual, we must equip them to be successful individuals, and these strategies are critical to our mission.

Critical Thinking: I Question, Therefore I Am

Alongside building a sense of self-worth in a child, we must teach young people to have the mental fortitude to withstand the attacks that are sure to come their way. I felt this fear when I was eight months pregnant with my first daughter. I had a panic attack. It suddenly occurred to me that not only would I be responsible for keeping this child safe, but that it was an almost impossible task. How could I keep her safe from *everything?* It seemed a problem that had no real solution short of some tower in a far off fairytale kingdom. Almost every day in the news we hear of atrocities against children. These sad occurrences have driven most parents to the point of creating walls—mental and physical—around their children in the hopes of protecting them from society's evils. We prevent children from scrapes and bruises with a barrage of bike-riding gear. We equip each child with low-jacked cell phones. Worst of all, we hover. We prevent the normal blow of a failed grade or a scrape on the arm. We even see these parents at the collegiate level. Can you imagine a professor having to discuss a grade with a parent when the "adult-child" could care less?

The instinct to hover is natural and, quite frankly, totally warranted in our society today. There are piranhas that lie in wait for an opportunity to hurt our children. A quick scan of any predator website will tell you that. Our only recourse as parents is to arm our children with an abundant amount of honesty. But the greatest weapon that you can offer your child is critical thinking skills.

Without the ability to logically decipher problems that will occur in the real world, and without the knowledge that the real world is very problematic, you are setting your child up for serious vulnerability. We have to work hard as parents to give our children the "what if" scenarios they will need to stretch their critical thinking.

Yet we do not equip our children with the critical thinking skills they need to survive in this society. Sadly, we tell children what they should and should not do. We leave no opportunity for children to grow and learn by failed choices, critical wisdom they will use in their teens as they venture out into the world. I'm not advocating that the consequence be severe, but children need to learn smaller life lessons that will help them solve their problems in the future.

Logical deduction is your child's greatest mental asset. Hone it well. If a child can figure out where a situation will eventually lead, how a current situation must have begun, and what to do to solve the problem in either case, there won't be anything society throws at them that they will not have some level of control over. Remember, our job as parents is to prepare our children to be productive members of society. They cannot do that if they are unaware of how to deal with both pleasant and unpleasant situations when they enter the world.

What Does It Mean to Critically Think?

Children need it and we want to give it to them. But what does it mean to think critically? I can give you a textbook definition. Critical thinking is "the mental process of actively and skillfully conceptualizing, applying, analyzing, synthesizing, and evaluating information to reach an answer or conclusion." I don't know about you, but there's got to be an easier way to define critical thinking. We've discussed having a critical habit of mind in earlier chapters, and I think those habits lead to strong critical thinking. Recall that having a critical habit of mind means

- removing your feelings from a situation,

- looking objectively (without emotions), and

- changing your opinion based on facts.

Removing your feelings, looking objectively, and changing your opinion when warranted. These are things a parent can teach at almost any stage of a child's development. Practice these skills with your children until you are sure that they have made a habit of thinking critically. I started with my girls when they were very young. Now, as they enter their preteen and teenage years, I can see the positive results. No, they are not perfect, but they do analyze situations—exactly what I need them to do.

Time for an Upgrade:
Ways to Boost Critical Thinking

As I said before, the easiest way to boost your critical thinking is to take a deep look at what you believe about the world and the people who occupy it. If you believe in treating people the way you want to be treated, does that include murder? And if so, why? Does your parenting reflect your belief in the child as an individual? How? Aside from deeply thinking about what you believe to be true about the world, there are more exciting (and kid-friendly) ways to boost your child's critical thinking (as well as your own critical thinking). Here are a few:

Practice logic problems. I added this section because logic problems really do help build stamina for long-term thinking. I also added them because they are my personal addiction; I adore them! Logic problems can be quite simple and fun. The key is whether you can figure out a solution based on given facts. Here are some logic problems that range from easy to downright perplexing. Have some fun trying to solve them![11]

Feeding Time

by Shelly Hazard

Zookeeper George was in charge of feeding all of the animals in the morning. He had a regular schedule that he followed every day. Can you figure it out from the clues?

The giraffes were fed before the zebras but after the monkeys.

---

[11]These logic puzzles are taken from Allstar Puzzles, at www.allstarpuzzles.com/logic/index.html and www.puzzlersparadise.com/puzzles/feedingtime.html. These are great websites to explore.

The bears were fed 15 minutes after the monkeys.

The lions were fed after the zebras.

	6:30 AM	6:45 AM	7:00 AM	7:15 AM	7:30 AM
Bears					
Giraffes					
Lions					
Monkeys					
Zebras					

Number Pyramid

A *Number Pyramid* is composed of the 10 different numbers 0-9 with a top row of 1 number resting on a second row of 2 sitting on a third row of 3 supported by a bottom row of 4. For example, a *Number Pyramid* could be:

0

1 2

3 4 5

6 7 8 9

Given the clues below, can you determine the composition of *Number Pyramid 9*?

The number on top the pyramid minus the sum of the two numbers in the second row equals 1.

The middle number in row 3 minus the number second from the right in row 4 equals 6.

The three numbers in row 3 sum to 24.

The leftmost numbers in the four rows of *Number Pyramid 9* add up to 24.

The rightmost number in row 4 minus the second number from the left in that row equals 3.

A Day at the Zoo

by Shelly Hazard

Can you find all the words in the word list in the grid below? The words can be found horizontally, vertically, diagonally, and backward.

One day, five mothers each brought their only child to the zoo. The children had a glorious time together watching the different animals and eating their favorite snacks. The kids were so good, at the end of the day each mother let her child get one item from the souvenir shop as they were leaving the zoo. Can you determine the full name of each child, each child's favorite snack and animal, and the souvenir each brought home?

Julia, who loves cotton candy, didn't like the elephants. Mary didn't get a caramel apple. The child who got the stuffed animal liked the giraffes best.

Alan Small, the girl who liked the lions, and the child who got the activity set didn't want to leave the zoo.

Neither of the boys got fried dough, but one got nachos and the other one liked the monkeys best. Tom didn't get a poster.

The Brown child almost got a coloring book with Mary but finally decided on a poster.

Tom, whose last name isn't Proctor, got a toy gun but didn't get a caramel apple. The Macgregor child had fried dough.

Beth, who didn't like the giraffes or the elephants best, got an activity set.

Use the grid to help solve the puzzle!

	Brown	Cook	MacGregor	Proctor	Small	caramel apple	cotton candy	fried dough	nachos	popcorn	elephants	giraffes	lions	monkeys	seals	activity set	coloring book	poster	stuffed animal	toy gun
Alan																				
Beth																				
Julia																				
Mary																				
Tom																				
activity set																				
coloring book																				
poster																				
stuffed animal																				
toy gun																				
elephants																				
giraffes																				
lions																				
monkeys																				
seals																				
caramel apple																				
cotton candy																				
fried dough																				
nachos																				
popcorn																				

The bottom line is that logic puzzles, easy or difficult, challenge you to look at how little things can affect a situation. They are not for everyone. I have friends who think my love for puzzles is weird. They simply can't get into the "logic puzzle rhythm." If you are one of those people, don't fret! Logic puzzles aren't the only way to increase critical thinking.

Teach your children to be their own problem solvers. There a few questions that I think parents should ask to help young people evaluate their situations and solve their problems and the first obvious tow are what is my problem? How can I solve it?

I tested this theory out on my daughter when she was quite young. She came to me and said, "I'm thirsty." I told her, "You have a problem. How are you going to solve it?" At first she looked at me like I was crazy. It was so much fun! After giving her some time to think about it, I said, "What do you need to do if you're thirsty?" It sounds ridiculous, but children need to be taught this self-questioning skill. If they can do this, they can self-answer—and keep others from answering for them! *We must teach our children to solve their own problems.* This is a skill every child can practice. When we send our children away from us—to school or a friend or family member's home—we are entrusting them to their own judgment. If their critical thinking skills are not developed, it will be easy for them to follow the crowd instead of having the courage to trust their own thoughts.

Analyze anything and everything. Simply taking the time to break a situation down to its smallest parts is a great way to boost critical thinking skills. Take your favorite book, subject, or political issue and ask yourself the following questions:

- Why do I agree with this point?
- Could there be reasons to disagree or dislike x, y, and z?

Listen to someone else's point of view on a subject. Why would someone believe that? Try explaining your point to someone who does not agree with you.

Before I moved to the less-liberal Midwest, I never thought about the value of the Second Amendment or the hard-won loyalty that some Americans have to the military. It offered perspective to learn other people's views and walk in their shoes. In some cases, my opinions were altered. In many, they were not. The point is not to force change. The point is to understand another's life experiences. That's what secular parenting provides: a way to see the world free of an entrenched verdict on a person that you've never met.

Ultimately, your job is to play the devil's advocate with your children. Teach them to see the opposite side of situations. This does not mean that their perspective is wrong or needs to be changed (make sure that your children knows that). It means that their decision should consider the various perspectives on a subject.

I'd like to end with something my husband wrote for our daughters. He wrote it out on a sheet of paper and hung it in our dining room. We read it to them once, talked about it, and moved on. I think it brings the idea of critical thinking into a complete package. It shows that with a critical habit of mind, lies cannot affect our worldviews, unwarranted emotions cannot delude our judgments, and the foolish actions of others will not fill us with contempt for them but instead remind us that there are still those who need a gentle guidance toward rational thought.

To have a critical habit of mind, we must be ready to

- think about new things, even if they don't agree with what we believe;

- admit that what we believe might be wrong, and if it proves to be wrong we must rethink our beliefs;

- change our beliefs so that they work with the facts that we learn about the world.

Our attitude must be one that is

- aware that all humans make mistakes sometimes and are wrong sometimes;

- open to other people's beliefs and just as ready to admit that they might be right as we are ready to think that we might be right;

- unwilling to assume that our wants help us to understand the truth about anything.

The skills we must work hardest on are

- understanding what we truly think about a belief and learning more about it if we realize that we don't understand it well enough yet;

- learning about beliefs we don't agree with in the same way and with the same attitude we use when learning about beliefs we do agree with;

- looking for and studying anything that may be wrong with what we are learning about.

—J.M.M.

5

Building a School of Tolerance One Parent at a Time

As we begin the conversation of school, tolerance, and secular life, it's important to note that the focus should not be on the school itself. People make a school. The culture of a school is defined by the greetings that a child gets in the hallways, the way administration treats their staff, and the support offered in a family's time of need. In looking at school and secular life, the culture of a school is critical. A welcoming school opens its arms to diversity because that is what Horace Mann, known as the father of public education, had in mind when he went about reforming American public education. A school drenched in old habits, on the other hand, will swallow the spirit of a secular family—of all families that deviate from its tradition, for that matter. The sad truth is that school wasn't initially created to be "the great equalizer."

The American public education system was initially created, as Jefferson put it, to "[rake in] a few geniuses from the rubbish." In the beginning, the vast majority of public schools relied almost exclusively on the *New England Primer*, the Bible, and the principles of Protestant Christianity to teach young boys. (Girls did not attend school past about third grade.) Our country soon realized the folly in mixing education and faith. When the dust settled around 1850, there were two school systems: the Catholic and the Public School System. These remain the two largest school systems today.

While the American public school system is supposed to be free of religious influence, recent lawsuits tell a different story:

In January 2012, sixteen-year-old Jessica Ahlquist of Rhode Island won a case against her high school to get a prayer removed from a wall in her school auditorium, where it had hung for forty-nine years.[12]

---

[12]Goodnough, Abby. "Student Faces Town's Wrath in Protest Against a Prayer." *The New York Times*. The New York Times Company. 26 January 2012. www.nytimes.com/2012/01/27/us/rhode-island-city-enraged-over-school-prayer-lawsuit.html?_r=0

A lawsuit was filed in May 2011 against Tennessee schools for excessive religious entanglement. Activities included the distribution of Bibles, prayer over the speaker system, and teacher endorsement of religion.[13]

A lawsuit was filed in South Carolina in 2009 over religious classes (taken at a church with no academic oversight) receiving high school credit.[14]

That last one is particularly cunning. Why not let students get credit for studying the Bible? Sounds good, right? Of course the answer is clear: Without oversight, how can one judge the "secular manner" of teaching?

We have organizations to help keep the "wall of separation" intact. In August 2012, the ACLU launched a preemptive strike against violations of the separation of church and state. The director of the South Carolina chapter said, "It's important [for] all students to know that they're going back to school to a place where they will

---

[13]Sun, Eryn. "Public Schools, Not Sunday Schools? ACLU Files Lawsuit." *The Christian Post.* The Christian Post, Inc. 2 May 2011. www.christianpost.com/news/public-schools-not-sunday-schools-aclu-files-lawsuit-50074/

[14] Barnett, "Ron. "Ruling lets S.C. students earn credit for religion classes." *USA Today.* USA Today. 3 July 2012. http://usatoday30.usatoday.com/news/education/story/2012-07-03/religion-courses-credit/55998826/1

be welcome no matter what they believe." It's clear that as America—and to a large degree, the world—becomes more religiously confrontational, the battle for education has also become hostile territory for the parents who haven't chosen the right side in the war. This is where our natural frustrations and fears come into play. We already know, thanks to Stephen Law, that there is a *War for Children's Minds*. His book made the case for strong, morally grounded children who can also think for themselves. That's what school *should* do for our children, and odds are, your child's school is already working toward that goal.

There is no reason to assume that your child's school—or the teachers that inhabit it—will have a decidedly negative response to you or your child because of secularist principles. Not only is it a poor way to begin a relationship; it also fails to consider a powerful alliance: *parent + school = the creation of a learned and civil member of society*. After years of working with young people, I can tell you there is a lightning bolt of wonder and creativity in a child when these two forces merge. But I also clearly remember the tinge of fear and the sense of repeated frustrations that I worried would come to pass. The same few thoughts went through my mind over and over again: *My daughter has no faith in a country where faith is sometimes all that matters, her mother is an atheist, and she lives in rural Missouri.* It took a conservative Christian, and thirty-year veteran of teaching, to remind me that not all the days ahead would be bad.

One day in the early fall of her kindergarten year, my daughter waltzed into the kitchen after school. She dropped her bag on the floor and, as she was running to the fridge, proclaimed, "Michael said I was going to hell today at lunch because I don't believe in God." Initially, I was more stunned by her nonchalant manner than by Michael's declaration. I did have a plan for talking to her about faith, but I'd hoped that would be further down the road.

I spent the next few days fuming, confused and hurt. I was sad for her, sad that my choice had made her life that much harder. That anger, in large part, fueled the start of this book. It also made me examine the best way to teach my child to combat the ignorance she was sure to face.

Introductions

A secular parent's first line of defense at school is always the teacher. In a perfect world, teachers would find ways to introduce themselves to you: a quick letter to sign, a welcome note, an email, etc. However, few teachers actually take the time to do this, so a quick email telling them who your child is and the best way to contact you is often a good start. That was wisdom I didn't possess at the time of Michael's incessant religious taunting.

Instead my husband and I talked about her feelings, what Michael had probably been taught, and how young children really should focus on learning instead of deciding who should get into heaven. I asked her if she wanted me to talk to her teacher. At first she said no. A few days later she changed her mind and I sent the teacher an email. Much to my surprise, my daughter's teacher was so shocked at this boy's insensitivity that she had the counselor intervene. Michael's parents were called. The harassment didn't end overnight. There was more than one occasion where Michael had crossed into "preacher mode": he took every available opportunity to remind Essence that her lack of faith made her different. Bad. That first encounter with religious intolerance in school would set the stage for many more. Through it all, I can say that it was the parent-teacher relationship that either saved the day or wrecked the whole affair.

I would loosely categorize parent-teacher relationships as either adversarial, alliance-based, or nonexistent. The most well-known, and unfortunately the most invoked, is first on our list.

Adversarial. This is when either the teacher or the parent has a hostile, uncooperative attitude. Whenever something happens at school it's either all the parent's fault or all the teacher's fault. See any problems with this logic?

Alliance-based. This is when both parent and teacher work together for the betterment of the child. There may be tension now and then, but both parties are willing to overlook this and focus on the student's needs at any given time.

Nonexistent. Here there is rarely contact between parent and teacher. Either the parent cannot get a hold of the teacher or vice versa. It may be bad timing or the failure of one side to create the needed time to focus. This does not mean that either side doesn't care; there is just a lack in communication.

Since our actions are in large part copied by our children, working to develop a positive relationship with your child's school will help students to develop positive attitudes about learning. After all, if you're cussing out the teacher after you get off the phone, you can hardly expect your child to go to school and have a high degree of respect for that teacher. Positive relationships with the school will also ensure that school is safe—mentally and physically.

A Day in the Life of a Teacher and a Parent

The first thing you should do to create a positive relationship is pat yourself on the back: By reading this—and any other parenting book—you are being the best parent you can. Now it is time to let your child's teachers know that! Parents and teachers are coming from two different points of view in terms of both the child in question and the school environment. We need to look critically at the relationship between parents and teachers. Who are parents? Who are teachers? Let's take a look at a small fragment of variables each group must deal with:

Parents	Teachers
• are the guardians of their child(ren). • may be single, married, divorced or widowed. • can be non-traditional: grandma, mom-mom, dad-dad, parent-partner, partner-partner, etc. • may have both caregivers working. • may have more than one child for whom they must provide. • may be upper, middle, or lower class. • may have a physically demanding job. • may not have time to read articles about researched-based methods. • may be confused about why a teacher is doing a particular exercise or activity with their child. • may not be able to adequately care for their child, despite their love. • probably have had poor experiences from their school years. • above all, love their child(ren).	• are responsible for the learning of 100 to 180 students at the middle and high school levels and 20 to 30 students at the elementary level. • are accountable for between 60 to 360 sets of parents (depending on the grade level), as well as administrators and school board members. • rarely have instructional assistance. • are probably stressed. • probably have up to a third of their students with special needs. • create and implement a state-approved curriculum. • may not have all the materials needed to teach successfully. • should have at least a bachelor's, and preferably a master's, in their chosen field. • are required to use researched-based methods for education. • may not have a livable wage.

This list, of course, could go on forever. But does it really need to? The fact is that teachers and parents are about as diverse as the amount of plant life on earth. As parents, we work hard to provide for our children. We may not have the same level of knowledge as teachers, but we care about education and future of our children more than most teachers will ever know. Teachers need professional development, accountability, pay that reflects their performance level, and, in most cases, a big pat on the back.

Before diving into conversations of religion with a child's teacher or principal, we as parents must build up our background knowledge on the subject.

What Does the Law Say?

The Constitution of the United States of America is an amazingly well-written, but kind of boring, document. The real fun things—the stuff that makes our country so interesting—are the amendments to the Constitution. It is here that we find how the law responds.

> **Amendment 1.** Congress shall make no law respecting an establishment of religion, or prohibiting the free exercise thereof; or abridging the freedom of speech, or of the press, or the right of the people peaceably to assemble, and to petition the Government for a redress of grievances.

This makes it illegal for our government to establish a "Church of America" similar to the Church of England. It also keeps public funds —funds that religious and non-religious people alike have contributed via taxes—from actively supporting religious establishments.

For public education this means that no school is allowed to sanction anything that directly advocates one religion above another, or any religious idea that is not related to the educational agenda of the curriculum. Also, educators are prohibited from creating a hostile atmosphere for students on the basis of their religion or lack of faith. Teachers can and should discuss religion in an objective manner, though this is usually limited to educational purposes only.

Sadly, our country has a horrible history with respecting this law. Many students—especially those in southern, rural areas and those in heavily religious communities—are subjected to religion in schools. This creates gray areas and leaves parents in a position of vulnerability. Do you raise the red flag when you notice that something seems off, or do move past it, pretending it didn't happen—in effect closing your eyes? There have been times where I wished my mouth could not speak of what my eyes saw. But we are right to root out unnecessary intrusions of faith, not out of malice, but out of a real intent to give our children a fighting chance at choice.

Determining True Violations

Before you decide whether or not something your child's teacher has done violates the separation of church and state, think about the three tests that are used to qualify or disqualify a teacher's actions:

The Lemon Test

Based on the 1971 case of Lemon v. Kurtzman, 403 U.S. 602, 612-13, the Court will rule a practice unconstitutional if:

It lacks any secular purpose. That is, if the practice lacks any non-religious purpose.

The practice either promotes or inhibits religion.

Or the practice excessively (in the Court's opinion) involves government with a religion.

The Coercion Test

Based on the 1992 case of Lee v. Weisman, 505 U.S. 577, the religious practice is examined to see to what extent, if any, pressure is applied to force or coerce individuals to participate. The Court has defined that "unconstitutional coercion occurs when: the government directs a formal religious exercise in such a way as to oblige the participation of objectors."

The Endorsement Test

Finally, drawing from the 1989 case of Allegheny County v. ACLU, 492 U.S. 573, the practice is examined to see if it unconstitutionally endorses religion by conveying "a message that religion is 'favored,' 'preferred,' or 'promoted' over other beliefs."

Our children suffer greatly when schools decide to add a biased view of religion to their programs. To be clear, I think it is vital that children over age ten study religion and religious doctrine. In order for them to decide if a religion is worth their support, they must learn about it. I do not, however, support the undermining of the school curriculum and environment so that religion can be viewed as "true." So what would you do if your child came home and said things that were not only false but obviously promoted religion or religious doctrine?

Can You Hear Me Now?
Communicating and Clarifying with Your Children

Creating good communication between you and your child's teacher means that you talk together in both good and bad times. Let's assume that you make such an effort and the following scenario occurs: Your son comes home from the sixth grade and tells you that his teacher said "evolution is a theory, not a fact. Nature is so complicated that it must have had a designer." This is an obvious reference to intelligent design (ID) and no matter what you do or do not believe, the evidence presented in court for intelligent design did not stand the test of objective scrutiny (By a conservative judge, no less). Instead of calling your local news station, first consider the options.

Only as a Last Resort: Calling the Principal

One thing you do not want to do is call the principal. No one likes it—especially effective principals—when you talk to administration before you actually talk to the teacher. A good principal is sure to ask first, "Have you spoken to the teacher about this? Did you and the teacher try to solve the problem?" Or, "What did the teacher say when you spoke to her/him about the situation?" Granted, a conversation with the principal will get the attention you want, but your relationship with the teacher—and, consequentially, your child's relationship with their teacher—will be forever damaged. As a teacher myself, I would be very frustrated if I was called into the principal's office about a problem that I didn't even know existed. How could I work to solve a problem if no one had told me he or she was uncomfortable about something I'd said?

The Real First Step: Gather All Possible Information

You will undoubtedly need to schedule a meeting with your child's teacher over issues of intolerance that need addressing. Before your meeting, you'll want to have documented as much as possible about what happened on the day in question: date, class period, what was said, what was being studied, how your child responded, how the teacher responded, etc. No one is on trial here, but having the facts of a situation will help all parties analyze things more objectively.

Positive Thinking: Assuming the Worst Benefits No One (Especially Not Your Child)

Because your child has told you something that they felt uncomfortable with does not mean that the teacher did it on purpose or that it is as severe as your child claims. Many teachers are confused about how far to go with religious conversations in class. They don't want to offend, but they also don't want to keep children in the dark. Likewise, children who are being taunted for something as personal as their family beliefs are sure to occasionally look through a misguided lens. Give the teacher the benefit of the doubt. Remaining calm and focused is the best way to enter into a meeting of this type, which might mean having the meeting three days later instead of one. Realize that you and the teacher—in most cases—want what's best for the *child*, not yourselves.

If you're uncomfortable with your child knowing anything about religion, you might want to rethink your views. In every school, religion comes up and is discussed. Religion is a part of the history and culture of our society; there's no escaping it. Besides, children need correct, objective knowledge in order to make a decision about their relationship with faith as they mature. Shielding them from religion won't help your child make an informed decision; it will keep them ignorant and in the dark.

The Meet-up: Potentially the Turning Point

A meeting with the teacher should be scheduled as soon as you suspect a violation of the establishment clause or some other law protecting your family's right to be free from religion at school. This is a no-brainer, and I'm not trying to insult your intelligence here. I only write it because how this meeting goes determines how the situation is dealt with. You should schedule a time that is convenient for both you and the teacher. Depending on the issue, you may also want the principal involved. Here is a good example of trying to deal with a frustrating situation in a calm and respectful manner—with the child in mind.

Second grade year, my daughter came home from school with a flag she had made during a Veteran's Day celebration. It was a typical school flag with one exception: Each white stripe had a fact about the United States and patriotism. One stripe read, "Our country which believes in one God." When she showed me her flag and I marveled at its beauty. I also reminded her that there have been lots of people in our culture who lived life the same way that we did. Believing in a God is not the only way to be a good patriot. We had a small family conversation (less than five minutes—no lecturing!) about the different faiths in America and about the reality of those who have no faith: Anyone is a patriot if they love, protect, and defend the basic principles of his or her country. This includes agnostics, pantheists, atheists, and pagans.

Essence was fine with the conversation, but I was still frustrated. Sure, I'd talked to my daughter about the issue, but telling a class of seven- and eight-year-olds that to be a patriot means to believe in one God made me uncomfortable. To solve this problem, I sent a letter to my daughter's teacher.

Dear Mrs. Smith, I wrote,

Essence recently brought home a flag project which read "Our one country which believes in God." It is this statement that is the subject of this email.

I am sure that you recall the letter that I wrote to you earlier this month letting you know that both I and my husband are atheists and that our daughter, Essence, is a godless child. She has no belief in god and, as she grows, she will acquire an understanding of god that is her own and her father and I will support that. That is why it was so shocking to see this flag project and to see that incorrect statement posted on it, not only for Essence, but for the rest of the children in her class and at Jones Elementary.

The first reason that it is shocking is because it equates a belief in god with loyalty to a country. This link is misleading and false. Our country was founded on enlightenment principles, which I am sure you are aware of. The founding fathers of this country—many of whom were agnostic, atheistic, and non-religious in general—sought to create a country that was not ruled by divine right, but ruled by the reason that man has been endowed by nature. That is why the Constitution has no mention of god or any other religious doctrine.

Another reason that this statement is misleading is the statement's accusation of patriotism. As an atheist, I consider myself 100% patriotic. I vote in every election, I pay taxes, I donate to charitable causes, I support the freedom and rights of others, I love and criticize my country (in the hopes that it will one day be the great nation that I know it is) and I have respect for the principles in which this country was found. I am an atheist and a patriot, Mrs. *Smith.*

Lastly, it is disturbing to see this level of religious indoctrination in a public school. There are almost 25 million Americans in this country who do not believe in God. This one line has the power to create a level of contempt in Essie's classroom not only for her, but for other American patriots who will be viewed negatively because of long-held and untrue beliefs about religion, patriotism, and country.

I thought it most proper to speak to you before speaking to anyone else at the school, especially since this occurred in your classroom. I do not want the intrusion of religion into my child's (or any other child's) schooling, regardless of the makeup of the community. I am well aware that the majority of this community is Christian and that you yourself, most likely, are Christian. It is not my position to be offensive toward any religion—most of my family is Christian. It is, however, my duty to see that the children of this country are not fed untruths and biased by such lines as "our one country which believes in God." I have noticed subtle religious statements in some of the things my children have come home with. For instance, there was a song where the last line "now hear the word of the Lord" was read. Please inform the music teacher that religious teachings at school are forbidden by law and I would appreciate it if she did not mix the two. There are plenty of children's songs that do not have religious undertones in them.

Before I end this email, I want you to know that I enjoy Jones Elementary very much. My children are happy and I feel the school is a safe and healthy place for them to be. This is due to the hardworking staff and wonderful students. It is my hope that this letter is not taken in offense because I consider you to be a superior teacher in all respects. I do not want Essence to be singled out by you, students in her class, or any other teachers/staff members in the building for our beliefs, and honestly I doubt that this will happen. There is no reason to single her out for classroom activities, because I am assuming that no intentional teaching of religious statements will be made in your classroom. I would love to meet with you to talk about this, and I am also aware that I missed Essie's parent-teacher conference. Perhaps my husband or I could meet/talk with you during your planning hour.

Thank you,

Be-Asia McKerracher

That letter may seem a bit strongly worded—and it was. Earlier that year, I'd sent a letter to the school about our "unique" family. I'd been having problems with the school's music teacher, who refused to stop having the children sing religious songs. After two incidents of this, and the flag issue, I needed to drive the message home. And it worked. I had a wonderful conversation with Mrs. Smith, who reminded me that she only had them do the assignment that way because that's how it was created in a pre-made teacher packet. This was understandable and made sense; teachers, especially elementary school teachers, have many resources that are prepared for them in advance and are difficult to alter. Mrs. Smith asked us what would have been a better way to communicate faith and patriotism. We told her to separate the two. Faith and patriotism can each stand alone. In the end, we had a wonderful conversation with her teacher because we were open-minded, she was open-minded, and our focus was on the child, not ourselves.

As long as what your child's teacher discussed was neutral, objective, and unbiased, religion in the classroom shouldn't be a problem. Remember, we do not want our children to have no knowledge of religion and its effect on our culture. We need our children to be exposed in a way that gives them factual information and allows them to judge for themselves whether or not religion's role was—and is—good. A much-needed class in our high schools is a history of religion class. This, of course, is hard to do without bias.[15] Let's take the teacher and classroom in the following discussion for example:

Teacher: So, we learned that even though Huck knew he was going to hell for not telling on his friend, he did it anyway.

Student: Maybe he didn't really believe.

Teacher: OK, maybe he wasn't particularly faithful.

Student: My pastor said that those who don't believe will go to hell.

Teacher: OK. Your pastor has a right to believe that. There are many views on what happens when you die, and in this class we will respect all of them. It is not my job to say which one is right or wrong. Do we have any other statements about Huck's decision to keep his friend free and risk being punished?

---

[15]What happens when a Christian teacher has an atheist child who says she doesn't believe in all this God stuff? Will the teacher say, "That's OK. You have that right"? Will the teacher allow other students to taunt the child into submission?

There is absolutely nothing wrong with this teacher's conversation. Now, a very religious person might see true fault here: *How can you tell my child that you will respect an atheist's right to believe that there is no God?* The answer to this question is very simple. As an educator I know that teachers must care for the feelings of all the children in their classrooms, not just the Christian children. When a teacher tries to put one faith above another, it is a violation.

Compare the objective teacher response above to a conversation that a teacher had with students in Kearny, New Jersey, in 2006. David Paszkiewicz told his history class outright that "those who do not accept Jesus will go to hell." This Baptist youth pastor *and* educator could not separate his duty to teach objectively the material he was given with the imperative put upon him to "advance the faith."

The teacher's actions not only condemned those students who were not Christians, it also had absolutely nothing to do with the history lesson he was teaching and was a waste of money and educational time—something our students can't afford to lose. So what if a discussion on religion does not necessarily equal an establishment violation because the teacher appeared to be objective? Here are a few things to consider when analyzing religious conversation in your child's class:

- What was the topic being studied and how did a conversation on religion further enhance the children's learning and understanding of the topic?

- If the topic had nothing to do with religion, how and why did a conversation on religion come up?

- Did the teacher allow both sides of the religious debate equal time, consideration, and respect? If not, why was one side privileged?

- Did the teacher's personal views on religion corrupt her or his objectivity?

- How does the teacher plan to avoid something like this happening in the future?

When you get together to meet with your child's teacher over a possible separation of church and state issue, it doesn't have to be a bad experience. However, no matter how uncomfortable it may be, you must advocate for your child. From here things can either get ugly or stay positive and neutral.

In the case of David Paszkiewicz, things got really ugly. Why? For starters, the school's administration was very religious and did not see the "harm" in Paszkiewicz's remarks. The Jewish parent who brought the complaint forward wasn't taken seriously until his son produced audio recordings that he'd made of class lectures, showing the flagrant things that Paszkiewicz had said. Even then, several weeks went by before the school district officials "took corrective action," but refused to disclose what that action entailed. The superintendent called David Paszkiewicz an excellent teacher despite the fact that he routinely used the first week in every semester to say things to children like:

[Jesus] did everything in his power to make sure that you could go to heaven, so much so that he took your sin on his own body, suffered your pains for you and he's saying, "Please accept me, believe me." If you reject that, you belong in hell.[16]

Why this man is still allowed to work with young children is beyond me. He deserves to lose his license. As educators, our job is to open young minds to the possibilities of the world. Mr. Paszkiewicz is an example of that duty gone horribly wrong. And if you're wondering, yes, it would be just as bad for a teacher that is an atheist (like myself) to take her job as an opportunity to show all the atrocities that have been done in the name of religion while showing none of the positive effects of religion on our society. There must be objectivity in our classrooms if we are to equip young children with the critical thinking skills they need to be successful in life.

---

[16]Kelley, Tina. "Talk in Class Turns to God, Setting Off Public Debate on Rights." *The New York Times.* The New York Times Company. 18 December 2006. www.nytimes.com/2006/12/18/nyregion/18kearny.html?_r=0

If you live in a town like Kearney, a place where atheists are a minority, you may want to consider some of the following ways to equip you and your child for what could be a serious battle in the halls of elementary, middle, or high schools.

Become active ahead of problems. Join the PTA, become familiar with the teachers that work with your child, and work to solidify relationships in the school. It is not necessary to ring the alarms by yelling, "My child is secular!" Remember, as far as the law goes, all children should be getting a secular education no matter their religion or lack thereof. This kind of subversive behavior seems a sad route to go: concealing oneself in order to build alliances. Let me assure you, it makes people truly reflect on their values when they've gotten to know you before judging you and are suddenly faced with a conundrum: You are simultaneously a good *and* non-religious person. (How can that be?)

Learn your school's policies. Often, people work at a school for so long that they simply forget there are codes for which the school is accountable. If there are no written laws against unwanted religious solicitation, the First Amendment is still on your side and every principal and teacher in that building knows it. The school district also has policies on religion, teacher conduct, and student rights if they receive public funding. Check these out as well.

Prepare your child. This doesn't have to be a lengthy conversation. I played the "What if?" game with our young girls. You could play it with children of any age. Simply ask, "What would you do if your teacher told you that you were going to hell or that you were bad because you didn't believe in your teacher's religion?" Give your child a way to handle the situation, mentally and physically. Instead of having your child feel horrible all day, your child should know that the *teacher* has done something inappropriate—not the child. Your child should feel comfortable talking with you about these issues. This only comes with frequent communication between you and your child.

Consider moving. I don't add this last one lightly. No matter where you go, there will be people who simply cannot change or are unaccepting of new ways of experiencing life. At the end of the day we have to ask ourselves a couple important questions: *Is living in this toxic environment worth it? Will moving to a new city, state, or country offer the end result that I'm looking for?* I've seen secular families move, struggle, and return. There are also many more that move and feel a sense of freedom that they could not find elsewhere. When we moved to northeast Missouri I was generally happy. The people were kind, the sunsets beautiful, and life was simple. But deep down I knew that the environment needed expanding. I knew we couldn't live there indefinitely so I began planning our life somewhere more diverse. I do not regret my decision—and if you move, don't regret it either. Embrace it, live it, own the choice and plan for it to succeed.

While I have labored on about preparing yourself for possible negative encounters, we must not forget those jewels that dwell in the valley of rocks. Most teachers have personal goals they want to accomplish and real lives that they lead outside of work. They enjoy working with young people and teaching their favorite subject. If you do come across a Paszkiewicz at your school and the district is giving you undue stress and not solving the problem, you have a couple of ways to handle the situation.

You could, of course, go large. The main reason Paszkiewicz was subjected to scrutiny was because of the publicity of the story. It comes at a price to be sure. The student that forced Paszkiewicz to comply ended up going to a different school. He was praised by some, taunted by most, and the administration certainly did not rescue that child from torment. That is why before you take a step like that, you must be sure there is no other way to deal with the situation.

A better avenue is to find an organization that will give you good advice about your specific situation and best options. Some that specialize in the religious breaches of a students' constitutional rights at school include

- American Civil Liberties Union
- Freedom from Religion Foundation
- American Atheists

These and many other organizations are committed to helping individuals who are pressured by other individuals or groups of people who refuse to follow our Constitution. You are not alone. American schools need not be a place of persecution and fear.

Another important thing to remember is that most schools do respect the separation of church and state. They work hard to make sure that all children feel safe, welcomed, and wanted. Many who work in education spend their evenings and weekends working on lesson plans. They fret about kids barely passing and work to provide for themselves and their families. There are rogue teachers, yes. These teachers do have agendas and will work hard to achieve them. Since many are sympathetic to faith, recruiting other teachers can be easy. But weeding out these educational pests can be done in a way that leaves everyone feeling good and your child feeling secure at school. Instead of assuming the worst, prepare for the worst—but give your school a chance to welcome you and your child into their family.

6

Merging Worlds:
Secularism and Loved Ones

One of the most difficult aspects of raising children "without God" is the arrows of frustration that family and friends can hurl your way once they have discovered your intentions. It can be very difficult to move through the scathing words to get at the heart of their sadness. This chapter is called merging worlds because that is really the key to maintaining positive relationships with more devout family and friends. We have to recognize their sadness, allow them time to grasp our resistance to faith-based parenting, and come up with a plan that leaves relationships intact.

I say this and yet I handled my own "coming out" very differently. I didn't understand that cooperation was the key; I was too busy being a proud secular parent to realize the damage I was causing. We were in my living room, senior year of college; I was graduating the next day. My mother and aunt had traveled from Seattle to Missouri and we had spent the last two days having a great time. Finally, my mother asked the question. She knew the answer, but she asked anyway: "Do you have a church that you guys go to around here? I know tomorrow's graduation, but if I stay until Sunday, I could go to church with you."

I could feel the heat around my ears, feel my arms warming to the sensation of anxiety and dread. Why did she ask it? My mother knew my thoughts on faith. She was also keenly aware of my parenting intentions. It wasn't that I wouldn't take my girls to church. I wanted them to be thoroughly grounded in reason before I did, and I knew they weren't there yet. So I tried to let her down smoothly.

"I'm not really religious these days," I said. A cop-out, I know, but what atheists want to talk about God with their mothers the night before graduation? My aunt sat calmly on the sidelines. She'd remembered my conversion from Christianity to Islam years back; she knew that I'd left Islam as well. This "new movement" didn't really faze her. She seemed to think that this too would pass.

My mother, on the other hand, had no understanding of such a progressive concept. She handled my response just as I thought she would. First, it was just a condescending "kids these days" attitude. But something inside of her began to swell up, then that something filled with a pain only anger could explain. She burst. My mother said plainly that it wasn't fair. How could I deny the right of these beautiful and perfect children to know the same Lord who had guided me to graduation's doorstep? From there things get blurry: tears, screams, yells of past grievances. Though sleep was rocky that night, the next day all was forgotten—until the question of faith and children seeped into another conversation down the road.

For family and friends, especially those of you "fortunate" enough to be in deeply religious circles, secular ideas can be extremely difficult, even impossible to talk about, but your story does not have to be similar to mine. The idea of secular parenting has matured over the last ten years, and you have the power to discuss secular parenting in a way that grants respect to both sides of the conversation. It requires that you do the exact opposite of my hostile decision. Before a discussion on secularism, separation of church and state, or any other nonreligious topic emerges, it is crucial that you and your partner look through the eyes of those who would condemn you most strongly. We don't have to *accept* their responses, but as critical thinkers we must try to *understand* them. We know that anger is always a secondary emotion; what precedes it is usually pain, hurt, and sadness.

As for my case, I waited, tormented myself with guilt, and separated my family from much-needed support and love. I had no skills for dealing with the outcomes of a "faith-based" conversation. I don't want this for any secular parent.

So what are the parameters of such a conversation? I held off speaking with my family about God for a few good reasons that I think most of us can relate to. I was raised a Baptist Christian and I can tell you that we didn't have a lot of books in our home, but the "Good Book" was always mounted somewhere special. It wasn't just that Jesus was plastered throughout my home—"He" was an integral and unquestioning part of my life.

As a child, the only certainty I had when it came to faith was that each week Jesus would meet me at his house, the Goodwill Missionary Baptist Church, to discuss the week's transgressions. It didn't matter if I'd stayed out till two a.m. the night before (and as a teenager I often did), I was still dragged out of bed, forced into clothes, and made to listen to the previous week's recycled sermon.

Religious devotion is a principle that was taught to us by way of tradition; we learned it as a fact before we were mentally capable of understanding what heaven, hell, or God, for that matter, really meant. Now that we have decided to turn against such doctrine, we must see our family not as enemies, but as people whose philosophy is fundamentally different from—and sometimes hostile to—ours. Per their understanding, God is not a myth or a belief, or even something to consider questioning: God is a living, breathing, complete and total truth; his reality is as veritable as the air in our lungs.

For many of our family members, their entire worldview might be wrapped in a neat little package called Islam, Judaism, or Christianity. This makes the idea of "secularism" quite toxic—and scary. Can you imagine your baby's baby—the future of your family—being denied the trusting arms of Christ, Muhammad, or Yahweh?

The feelings of betrayal and sadness would be very real for you. That is why we take conversations about secular parenting seriously—they set the tone for both your child and future familial relationships. So how does one begin?

Fire and Brimstone: That Used to Work, Right?

As with all parental decisions, options abound. The first is easy: *condemn and purge.* They deserve it, don't they? These are the people who have been completely dishonest. They sold you not so much a lie, but a half truth. My friend James went that route. When he found serious inconsistencies in his religion, he promptly became an agnostic. Further reading led him to ask parents, friends, even his pastor, "Why didn't you tell me . . . ? And so what about . . . ? Did you know that . . . ?"

The conversation went on for weeks. Eventually everyone stopped talking. Ultimately, James was angry and his children were denied the right to visit their grandparents. What exactly did that accomplish? You've robbed yourself of an ally in the fight to raise healthy and happy children, and you've stolen a chest of unconditional love from your children. This section—condemning and purging—is small because it should be. This is simply a bad option.

Sadly, this story is repeated all too often. Conversations about secularism are life-altering and will forever change the dynamics of your family. But try to remember that this is a good thing. If we are intent on living in a society where everyone is respected, and everyone feels they belong, then we must address the issue of religion and young children head-on. Why? Because change begins with the youngest in our society. If we teach children to love regardless of faith then they will love no matter a person's faith. If we teach them to hate based on whose God is most correct, they will honor our legacy with hate.

It will be heart-wrenching for many of your family members to learn that you are choosing a secular way of life. Of course, for your more open-minded family members, curiosity might replace anguish. I had a cousin once ask me, "So why don't you believe in God? You went to church every Sunday like me." Her tone was not angry; she just wanted to know the reasons behind my choice. Most of us will not get such wonderful responses, but, in the end, being true to your family's secular lifestyle is the best way to set an example for your young citizens. How can this be done the right way?

My husband and I have done hours of reading, talking, and thinking. We have determined that organized religion is not appropriate for our girls at such a young age; they need time to develop their critical thinking skills. They also need more life experience before they dive into organized faith. Since my mother lives two thousand miles away, religion rarely surfaces in daily conversation. You may not be so lucky. If you cherish your relationship with your family members these conversations will be all the more difficult.

Do we regret our decision raise our children with strong critical thinking skills, even to question religion? Absolutely not! Christianity makes sense for my in-laws and my parents; they have that right. But I have learned that religion is not necessary for raising a morally healthy child; religion is not the choice for my small family, and my husband and I have that right too.

Coming Out of the Secular Closet

Whether you are reading this book as an atheist, agnostic, or simply a nonreligious person who wishes to raise a secular child, I urge you to consider the manner in which you discuss your decisions with family and friends. Whatever your choice, you must be willing to ensure that no adverse behavior be tolerated by family members. Let me say that another way: *Subversive behavior by family and friends is categorically unacceptable.*

With that said, you have the right to choose what is best for your children without guilt or remorse. Whether you tell your family lightly or matter-of-factly, be prepared to stand your ground respectfully and lovingly.

As you begin to consider secular parenting as a conversation, I would encourage you to do some self-reflection. Start by asking yourself, *What is my goal here?* Every meaningful conversation that you have has a desired outcome. What's yours?

Do you want family unity? There's no denying that it would be nice to see family and feel a sense of connection that may be missing because of current religious frustrations. It takes time, but that feeling will return, and if that's your goal, go for it!

Do you simply want your family to agree to disagree when it comes to religious differences? You know your family best. It might be that no matter the conversations, no matter your patience, your parents, grandparents, aunts, uncles, etc. will *never* be willing to look past the differences you share. In this case, the only real option is to find ways to end conversations on faith as soon as they begin. Sure, you will have a conversation "coming out," declaring the boundary lines, and announcing love—but that might be it.

Are you perhaps looking for eventual, deeper, "monumental" conversations about the role religion has played in your family? Getting to this stage can be painful; in my own family it took several patient conversations that ultimately went nowhere. The end result was the reality that religion had scarred some of the bonds in my family in way that will never heal. I do not regret the journey to that reality, and neither should you. The question that immediately follows is, *Are you ready to move on?* Moving past and learning to heal can take many forms: isolation, emotional distance, and even anger. Just like dealing with a loved one who has died, religious walls built deep inside a family structure cause everyone to grieve once they begin to fall. The good news is that, without those walls, things become clearer, more meaningful; existing bonds tighten and life does move on.

If you decide to let "secular parenting" come up whenever and wherever—which is similar to what we did—be forewarned, you are on route for a potential blow-up in the store, at the movies, or in another public place. I will admit the shock on the faces of some family members was met with slight excitement on my part. I loved the endless conversations about whether I was right or wrong; I felt empowered by my rejection of religion, and I wanted to make my case. You may not enjoy such events. For many, arguing with loved ones, even without yelling, can be very unnerving. An alternate way is to open up dialogue in a place of your choosing and in a controlled manner.

Have a family meeting. I like this option, and when I talk to people who have chosen it, they agree. Your mother, father, and siblings love you more than anyone on this planet—they will listen to a sincere and well-thought-out pitch. You can be very formal by reading something you've prepared in advance. This will also give you a chance to run through potential questions and rebuttals; you can have responses ready. This meeting doesn't have to take place in "the lion's den" either. You can meet for brunch or for dinner. Meetings are flexible, so put some thought into your decision. Ultimately, the formality can also help you explain how you came to your decision and provide the opportunity for you to ask that, in spite of your secularism, that your family love and respect you and your decision. In all cases, I would suggest leaving the kids with a sitter—this is an adult conversation!

Write a letter or send an email. If you've thought about a conversation but cannot foresee a scenario where it ends with your main goal in mind (or if the idea of a "conversation" causes stress) then option number two is for you! This is by far a better solution than the face to face arguing and streaming tears you're sure to encounter by the more vocal members of your family. Call me a wimp; I don't care. We only have so much time on this planet, and I'd rather not spend it arguing with anyone, least of all those I love most. After the graduation ceremony, and seeing my mom off at the airport, I did regret some of my former happiness. Yes, the ten-year old in me wanted to yell and scream, and for a time I let her do just that. Eventually I did write that letter. I wanted my mother to know that atheism wasn't a random event. It was a journey. I assured her that my goal wasn't to create two more atheists for the "Atheist God." I wanted my children to have a say in their faith and to give them a real chance at choice. I could not favor her faith above others.

The letter that you write won't be a crawling back into the closet. It will be an affirmation of choice, a hand of love extended. It is the reader's choice to reach out and grab the olive branch. *No matter the outcome, parents have a right to raise their children the way they feel is best.* Guilt is not one of the tenets of creating a free-thinking child, and if you raise your child the way your parents want you to because they make you feel guilty, you will be doing yourself and your child a huge disservice. You both deserve better.

Hide it from your family. My father-in-law was a Baptist minister for thirty years before he passed away. A "born again" Christian, he traveled not only in America but through Germany, Scotland, and England preaching God's love. He was well-known and well-respected. And while he was aware of our lack of devotion, we never really came out and denied our faith in his presence. The response to such a conversation or a letter would have been nuclear.

Couple his years of devotion with his severe medical and mental issues, and you have some serious decisions to make.

It would be wise for us as secular individuals to really consider the benefits *and* the drawbacks of conversations with loved ones, especially those in their most senior years. I would never advise hiding who you are (unless you felt your lives depended on it), but I would say this: If the benefit does not outweigh the potential fallout, why cross that bridge? Although my father in-law had spent well over sixty years of his life earnestly believing and preaching the Gospel of Jesus, he rarely brought up faith around the children and they did not attend services with him. My husband and I had a hard time convincing ourselves that putting him through such an ordeal—when we knew we didn't have much time with him—was worth my father-in law "knowing" about our decision. So we didn't tell him.

Although you may take due time and diligence trying to choose the best method to speak with your family about your secular lifestyle, they may need some time to process the information. Secular parenting is a direct affront (in many cases) to the way that we were raised, and family and friends will need time to sift through their anger and frustration.

My younger brother is a perfect example here. While I converted to the Nation of Islam in my younger days, my brother moved from

Christianity to Orthodox Islam. While this may take several forms (Sunni, Sufi, etc.) it was my refusal to believe in a God, any God, that was his source of frustration. My brother and I were very close—quite inseparable in our youngest days. So it was quite a blow to learn that, after he spent three years trying to convert me to Islam, he had decided he could no longer associate with me—permanently. He told my mother that my body—my soul—was a vessel for Satan that I refused to keep barricaded by faith. Not only me, but my children had fallen victim to this lowest of blows. He would not associate with my daughters nor allow his children in our lives. In one fell swoop I'd lost my brother, my nieces, and part of who I was. To this day he refuses to speak with me or my children, and my mother's solution is to (gently) request that I give faith another try because all of my success in life "came from the man upstairs."

It's no secret that in many ways, exposing your secular lifestyle to family and friends will cause grief. We are sometimes made to feel guilty or wrong for taking the road less traveled. Many secularists initially feel anger toward our religious family. We want to know why our feelings were—consciously or unconsciously—suppressed by those around us. How was faith allowed to be the only way? It is normal to feel a loss of precious time that we cannot get back.

That is why allowing your children to choose what will guide their lives is so important. I want to congratulate you and reassure you that your decision is the right one. Allowing your children—and perhaps you yourself—to choose what religion, if any, will guide their lives is a splendid gift. Many adults wished they could have had such a gift as children. We know as parents that every decision we make has consequences. Before discussing things with your family, ask yourself,

Do I know why I want a conversation with family or friends? What is my goal in having these conversations?

Is there anything going on in my family that might make this conversation more stressful for everyone? (For example, a recent death in the family, a terminal illness, or hardships in general.) There's no need to spring such a consequential decision on a grieving family. If there is any room for time—time for healing, grieving, and renewed bonds—you should be patient.

How will I deal with those family members who are not accepting? Like my brother, you must have a plan focused on family unity. That is always the end goal.

What sort of rules will I have regarding religious instruction, church, and other religious conversations with respect to my children? For example, how will you deal with family members who tell your children they (or you) will burn in hell for this evil, or that you are raising your children to hate God? This is an unfortunate reality in extreme cases. You will know whether or not to expect such responses from your family.

How will you prepare your children for your family's reaction? A bit more on the last question is necessary. Children should know how others may feel about their way of life. This is important for several reasons. First, children must learn that there are many ways to live and that no one way is the "right" way. Discussing your family's views can only cement the idea that different is not bad—after all, you're a perfectly normal person and you have thoughts that are not mainstream, right? Also, children must understand that close-minded people do exist. Your child has a right to have their beliefs respected whether someone agrees with them or not.

We were very honest with our children and I think you should be too. We told them that some people might be upset because they strongly believe in their religion and questioning it is not something they are taught to do. I told them that they have a right to question things that don't make sense to them. We tell them, often, that

They have a right to think and feel the way they do.

No one should make them feel bad about what they think or feel if they aren't hurting themselves or anyone else. Not Grandma, not Auntie, not even Mom or Dad!

They have a right to *not* talk about God or religion if they don't want to.

The last statement is very important. Often, people will badger secular-minded people into discussing and making a choice about their understanding of the world. Sadly, people will do this to children, too. Can you imagine an adult constantly badgering your child because they want to change your child's mind? I tell my girls that they have the right to (respectfully) say, "I don't want to talk about this right now and my mom said that if I don't want to talk about it that I don't have to."

We also tell the girls to let us know if they feel uncomfortable because of what an adult is saying about them or their family. Give your children the tools to stand up to the pressure of others. Teach them to defend themselves and others from rogue attacks because of their worldview. Bullies come in all sizes.

These skills are very important for young children to have because they chase away feelings of fear that can come up as a result of being intimidated by adults and peers alike. Remember Essence and her first grade friend-bullies? These statements should be posted where your kids can see them, or at least discussed often so children feel comfortable using them. Role playing works very well. I pretend to be an angry adult and they get very good at not being afraid of adult intimidation.

My goal here is not to offer a play-by-play of what to do. This is difficult stuff and the best idea is to have many conversations with your significant other, yourself, and your children until you come up with a plan that works for your family. If you can answer the questions I asked you earlier, and if you practice preparing your children for peers and adults who may take advantage of their youth, I think you will have prepared your family well.

It is also true that these types of core family belief issues can divide a family. It is important to let your extended family know that, no matter what, you love and appreciate them and their concerns. You can discuss things all you like and, of course, if you come to different conclusions, you should rethink your decision. But if you feel your decision is the best, you have every right to follow through—in defiance of family members who don't agree— because in the end you are responsible for sending your children into the world as mature, moral young people.

7

Religious Texts, Places, and Spaces

There is no way to raise a well-rounded, productive member of society *and* keep your child separate from religious texts. This seems to be more of an unintended consequence of secular life rather than something we as secular parents do on purpose. Well over seventy percent of Americans believe in something spiritual. If our children are going to have a shot at success, they will need to know those stories as well. **This means that you have to be on the lookout for ways that faith may be misinterpreted.** The best way to do that is with the text itself.

"Holy" Text?

The debate about whether or not a holy text is worthy of such a title is an argument I welcome, but I will not address this in a parenting book. What your child needs to know is that those who follow Buddhism, or Christianity, or Islam, believe that their text *is* holy. I've repeatedly told our children that I do not believe any text is holy because I don't. But that doesn't give me the right to demean or disrespect a book that others may see as such. Do I kiss the Quran that is on my shelf and wrap it in clean linen? No. Do I place the Bible on its own special, coveted altar in my home? No. Both books are on my shelf and treated with the same respect that I do all books. I do, however, recognize the significance that devoted individuals place upon these books, and I am careful to encourage conversation and respect as we discuss their contents with my children.

Remember: Respecting isn't the same as validating. I will respect any holy book, and I teach my children to do the same. That in no way means that what is contained in those books is true or that it is something I must hold dear.

When you have a young mind and an ancient text, you have to seriously consider how the two might fit together. In America, we crush our religious texts with the weight of our devotion; sadly, we often crush our critical thinking skills in the process. However, in this area children have made our process simple: Helping your child discover any religious text should follow the natural maturity and questioning that your child presents. Whether they have an interest in religion or not, it is your responsibility as the parent to offer proper, unbiased exposure to the faith that dominates your culture. This should be done mainly because you want your children to be successful in their environment. Being religiously literate is a major part of that.[17]

My husband and I began religious instruction with those principal Biblical tales that encapsulate any Sunday school upbringing. We chose stories from the Bible that are overrepresented in writing, television, movies, and songs. For a basic foundation in Bible stories, I'd recommend:

- Adam and Eve
- David and Goliath
- Jonah and the big fish
- Cain and Abel
- Noah and the flood
- Sampson and Delilah

Bible stories are easy to describe and they offer a window into some of the basic principles of the Christian faith. They are easily retold, and asking children their thoughts about these classics is just plain fun! My oldest daughter loved the story of David and Goliath and asked me to tell it to her every night before bed for at least a

---

[17]This book focuses on Christianity as it is the dominant faith in America. You may use the same method substituting the dominant faith in your area for the Christian faith.

week. She wanted me to change the name because she was a girl so could stand up to big ol' Goliath! If you are particularly creative parent (sadly, I am not), you can take an animated approach and reenact Bible stories, you can take a more measured approach and simply tell the story, or you can go somewhere in between.

Many of the secular parents I've spoken with are unsure about the use of an actual Bible stories book. Typically the images are not culturally diverse (and I believe that children should see themselves in some of those pages) and the goal of a Bible stories book is to indoctrinate for the purposes of belief. Call me paranoid, but I learned more actually reading the stories out of the Bible and then talking with my children about them. We drew them out on paper occasionally, acted them out once, and my kids got a chance to see it from their perspective as often as possible. I'm not so sure they would have done the same with a Bible stories book.

Keep in mind that exposure does not equal fact either. We had so much fun with these stories. Then one day my daughter asked if they were real. Did Cain really kill his brother? Did every living creature on the planet really fit on Noah's boat? Her friend had told her they were more than stories. Be prepared for this question! There is certainly no proof of Cain or Abel. No boat built today could house every living creature on the planet, so could that have happened so long ago? You will need to use logic and reasoning to help your child navigate. There is a lot that we can learn from a Bible story, but at the end of the day, many of the Bible stories sit in a sort of limbo: fiction peppered with historical facts.

We began introducing our children to organized religion between the ages of four and five. This was a good age because the first conversations are about those basic questions and help children outline the arguments for and against belief in supernatural places and people. By the time our children were in kindergarten, Bible stories became an ongoing conversation. This wasn't overly systematic, and I suspect it won't be in your home as well. We have way too much to do as parents—the last thing we need to add is religious instruction! Does it really matter if your child knows every story on the list? Are you then a bad parent if they can't recall a story on command? Of course not. The point isn't to memorize the books of the Bible. However, it was something that we spoke about often because we wanted it to help our children navigate the community they lived in, which entailed that they get the gist of the most popular stories of the Christian scripture. Finally, we wanted our girls to know that no matter what they felt about the stories, they needed to know that "lots and lots of people believe they are true, and that matters."

As children age, they can take on the challenges of "meatier" Bible tales. There are some pretty great stories in the Bible, and there are others that defy belief—and not in the spiritually uplifting sort of way. A secular parent doesn't have time to shy away from the reality of sex. One Bible tale that sparked real conversation came when my daughter was twelve. When the news brought up gay marriage, we aired our views on the subject. Then the story of Lot came to my husband's mind, so he told her the story from Genesis 19. Poor Lot: He offered the oversexed mob that stood outside his doors his virgin daughters to rape—instead of the two (male) angels that came from Heaven to visit him that day. In that way, homosexuality must be stopped, even if it means stripping young girls of something as precious as their virginity. My daughters had very interesting things to say about the holiness of Lot's actions. They did, however, find a sort of heroine in the book of Esther, and so did I. From that tale, they felt that Esther was "super brave," choosing to face death by visiting her husband, the king, in defense of the Jewish people. Granted, that tale isn't all cookies and roses, but knowing about Esther shows my girls an example of strong determination in a woman with considerably less rights than we enjoy today.

In addition to becoming familiar with the stories in the Bible, *a secular child needs to understand the connection to culture that exists within all religious texts.* We can learn much about the cultural norms of our ancestors. Yes, many of the practices are archaic, outdated, and sometimes even barbaric. But that is just the point. You and I—as adults—have made these connections; young people should be exposed to historical texts so that the opportunity to explore the past, and its relation to the present, can be fully realized. If the Bible, the Quran, and other religious texts are to be a template for life, then those texts must be broken down and analyzed in as many ways as possible. Ultimately, this begins with simple, short conversations about faith.

However, be sure to guard against lecturing. If your conversation has you talking more than your child, chances are they've lost interest and you need to wait until the next opportunity.

Religious Spaces and Places

My first memory of church is really one of awe. The walls were draped with softly sculpted angels that looked like infants and toddlers. The windows were so full of color that it took me several seconds to piece together the image. Candles illuminated the room. And when I looked at the ceiling, it was the most beautiful picture I'd ever seen: Each section of the ceiling had a story. There were swords in some, animals in others. Some of the images had positive connotations and others were downright frightening to my young mind.

I had so many questions about those images: Could any of the angels ever be black? Why don't we have colored windows at our house? Why is he speaking another language? What is a Bible? Of course, those were questions that had nothing at all to do with my aunt's funeral, so they weren't answered by any adult in the room. In the end, it wasn't the best way to introduce a young critical thinker to a new environment. It left unresolved questions in my mind and provoked serious confusion that was never really addressed.

So when should parents introduce organized religion to their children? We cannot plan the death of loved ones or any other random event will lead us into a house of worship, and we shouldn't try. The answer to this will depend on

- the age of your child,
- your personal comfort level with the religion in question, and
- the depth to which you are willing to explain religious practices and customs.

When my daughter expressed interest in Buddhism for a school assignment on world religions, she created a PowerPoint on the subject. This required her to go to the library, check out books, read the books, synthesize her information, and then come to her own conclusions. She was so excited! Every day we were given a small taste of the Buddhist faith by our resident Buddhist scholar. At the end of it all, we would have liked to take her to a Buddhist home of worship, a culminating experience, but life happened. She was eleven when she began the journey of learning more about Buddhism, a perfect age for such endeavors.

Initially, children should begin their journey toward understanding faith with an exchange of knowledge between the two of you. This should definitely take place before a child goes into a church. Before my girls went into a church, we took time to talk about the reverence given to the place of worship that we were to visit. I wanted them to know that during the time they will be going into the church, it will be a focused time. They could not play. Later, when the girls visited another church during Sunday school, we talked about the fact that there was playtime and crayons, circle time and treats.

When a child walks into any new space, like a place of worship, they will undoubtedly have some of the same questions that you or I had. During a first journey to a place of religious worship, we as parents become teachers. Good teachers try to help their students cement ideas in their minds through a mix of questions and observations. *This is an important step that should not be skipped!* These questions, of course, will depend on the age of the child, but they will probably look something like this: *Why do you think a church has windows like that?* Or, *why do you think the area closest to the pastor is higher than where we sit?* The goal is to connect what a child knows already with what they are seeing. It's such a fascinating thing to participate in! I love when children are stretching their minds, making room for more ways of thinking. This can be done, of course, in any setting, but it is particularly useful when in a new environment.

When my mother was made aware of the fact that we were raising our children minus "the church," she asked two questions: 1) Why don't you let the children go to church and experience God for themselves? 2) Why don't you let them make up their own minds? (Sigh.)

This line of thinking is a real false dichotomy that so many parents find themselves confronted with. I think we can all agree that when you go to a church—any church—the ultimate goal isn't for you to make up your mind about God. Church is for worship. Hence everything about the experience should pull a person toward loving God. There is a time and a place for children to go to church. This is where my nostrils flare. A child's first experience with organized religion should be taken seriously and should definitely include you as the parent. Unfortunately, it's just too easy for others to botch the job and for the parent to miss out on critical interactions and observations and talk about their thinking afterwards. Of course a few musts are involved first. Your children should:

- have a grasp on the faith involved (in order that they may see with their eyes open),
- be interested in going,
- and be at an age where they can use their knowledge and understanding of the world to express their thoughts and feelings.

In general, eight or nine is a great time to begin introducing children to religious spaces. A more conservative parent on the subject, I waited until my girls were ten and eleven and it went well.

Another question parents should consider is, "What are the rules once you get there?" One of my early memories of church involved the "eating of the flesh and drinking of the blood" ritual. I *really* wish someone would have prepared me for that Baptist tradition! Not only did I ruin the ceremony for all of the people who were there, I felt embarrassed and confused. Instead of just taking the cracker and drinking the juice, I was trying to figure out why were supposed to eat God's only son. How would *that* make God love me? Remember, in a context such as this, parents are critically evaluating not only the environment, but the effect the environment will have on their child's understanding of faith. My children would not participate in a ritual that requires cannibalistic activities. Period. For other free-thinking parents, the participation in a ritual like this might be a way of opening a dialogue on cultural practices of the past and whether or not it has relevance today (and whether or not that relevance has morphed from its original intention).

My children did participate in the ritual that required them to help those in need by adding money to the collection plate. I wanted them to see that positive aspects of faith do exist. In doing that, I could talk with them about the fact that we non-Christians also donate. A logical deduction might be then that anybody can donate; donating is not something limited to a religion.

Now, if you have a two-year-old experiencing a house of worship for the first time, chances are they simply will be irritated at having to sit for long periods and listen to some person speak. Preschoolers and school-aged children will most likely have many questions which will require your guidance. They will also be heavily influenced by the people they meet and the tone of the establishment—and they're ridiculously squirrely! Pre-teens and teens will be in the best position to judge what they are seeing with the years of learning about religion they have acquired from you. It is for that reason that I strongly recommend that children not attend religious services before age ten. This is, of course, a personal and parental choice. No matter your decision:

You must give your child a strong foundation in critical thinking before you expose them to organized religion and religious practices. Since religion has the ability to dictate how one lives one's life, children must be allowed to question, to no end, the rules and regulations that they must follow for the religion in which they are interested. Without critical thinking skills, your children will not be able to analyze the new information presented to them. They may take in what they see at face-value, develop fears, and become close-minded to other interpretations.

Children should have a basic overview of the religion and how it affects the lives of those who believe in it. When we began to introduce the religion of Christianity to our children, we gave a brief overview of who God is supposed to be, what the Bible is supposed to do, and why we think differently. It took several short conversations over a period of time. The conversations went something like this: "There are lots of people in this world who believe in something called God. God is *supposed* to be the thing that made people, plants, animals and even the stars. There are lots of religions—that means 'ways of thinking about God'—that give God different names, like Allah, Yahweh, or just God. There are even people who believe that God is a man or a woman."

Then we took the time to give them an overview of the major religion in our area (Christianity). I should say that it was a very much abbreviated version: "The Bible is a book of rules that tells people how to live. It is supposed to be written by people who speak for God. It says a man named Jesus, who is God's son, lived a long time ago. He said that it was his job to die so that people could get to Heaven—but only those people who followed the rules that he made would be allowed into Heaven. When Jesus died his soul (another conversation) floated out of the ground, through the sky, and up into Heaven, where God is *supposed* to be. Everyone who didn't follow the Bible went to a place called hell where they were in pain for not believing."

Finally, we gave our kids our reason for not believing in God, heaven, or hell. We also told them that if they choose, when they are adults, to believe in Christ, we will be happy for them. In one way or another, I tell my children:

I do not believe that Jesus died for me or anyone else. No one can die for you. We all die one day for ourselves.

Heaven is not a real place for me because when I look into the sky, all I see are clouds and stars. People have traveled to the moon but they did not see heaven. We have many satellites that have not picked up the sounds people should be making in heaven. We have looked all through our solar system (as far as we can), and there is no proof that heaven is out there. So *for me*, it is not a real place.

For me, God is not real. Even though this is something I believe, that isn't something you have to believe. God can be real for you.

Your job right now as a child is to think about everything that you learn and decide what makes the most sense to you when you are an adult. You get to choose.

I am never rude or unkind to someone who does believe in God. That is how they see the world, but I have a right not to believe in God.

No one should make you feel bad if you do not believe in God. You don't have to believe if God doesn't make sense to you.

Your reasons may be different and that's OK. *The only rule here is that you are honest and objective when you discuss religion, belief, and your feelings.* Did you notice the phrases like "some people," "I believe," and "for me"? This is important because I want my children to know that people do think differently and that neither these people nor their way of thinking is bad.

At first, my husband and I felt like perhaps we were telling our children something wrong. Having come from religiously strict backgrounds, we simply had no experience talking openly and honestly about our feelings toward religion. You may feel this way too. But the truth is that you are preparing your children to be healthy skeptics of life. You are giving them the gift of a balanced point of view, and you should be congratulated. The conversation of religion should be an ongoing one, discussed as questions and life examples arise. *It is important to let your children know that no matter what religion they attach themselves to, they will not lose you as their parents.* As an atheist, it would be difficult for me to see my child believing in any religion, honestly. But I would love them nonetheless because they are not me, because I have chosen atheism, and because my job isn't to create more atheists. My job is to help an individual learn to be a productive member of a diverse society.

Once your children have strong critically-thinking brains and a working overview of the faith in question, allowing them to participate in a religious function becomes an active learning experience. Remember: This is not a requirement for your child to be cultured, "normal," or any other such descriptor. Your child *can* learn about religion without actively participating in it.

But what about a sense of community? Don't religious spaces bring people together? Consider this:

You get a knock on the door and two teenage girls are standing there. They say they are from the local Christian summer day camp. Your child is invited to spend an afternoon singing songs, playing games, eating candy . . . and learning about God. They leave a flyer with the address and phone number for this free program. Would you let your child attend? What is your rationale for saying "yes" or "no"?

As secular parents, we want our children to understand the culture they live in, and that certainly means exposing them to religion in *some* form. So after reading this scenario, I invite you to think about the following questions:

If candy, fun, and games equals God, will my children not think critically about what they are learning?

Will my children learn about the good and bad aspects of religion, or will they think only of the happy people, the balloons, the snacks, and how badly they'd love to visit that place again?

Will my child agree to love God because it's fun? If so, is that a good reason to believe in God?

I would not allow my children to attend the summer camp and learn about God at that time and in that manner. Why? Because God shouldn't be for sale. Groups, by their very nature, need members; groups are pushers of ideas. The only way to get new members is to entice. Now, groups and members are good things—for people who can look past their advertising and see what they're really selling. For example, if you want to support breast cancer you can buy a pink ribbon. If you're also buying the ribbon because it will look nice on your car, then you are buying it because of its looks *and* because you understand and support the organization that you're giving your money to.

Our children don't have the luxury of a finely developed critical habit of mind. They will see pretty colors, nice people (who will tell them how beautiful and special they are) and be told how much God loves them. It is a biased sort of recruitment that is almost guaranteed to work. We as freethinking parents owe it to our children to present religion more objectively. This is something that we must get right, and there aren't many do-overs if we make a mistake.

Youth groups, with respect to most religions, are designed to seem fun and to "attract" young children and keep them through adulthood. They are deceptive by nature and they do not promote a healthy skepticism about religion. They do not promote active, critical learning. They lull children's brains to sleep with candy, songs, people who will dote on them, and a wholly inaccurate way of looking at religion, death, and the mysteries of life.

I say all of this knowing about the Great Girl Scout Fight of 2007. That's when both my girls wanted to join the Girl Scouts and I swore it would be over my dead body. There would be no putting of my children in an organization that said prayers multiple times a day *and* actively discriminated against the LGBTQ community. But they really wanted to. I played my part, parceling out information on the Girls Scouts for a couple weeks. The children worked hard to convince me that, despite all its faults, they wanted to be a part of it. So I said they could go to the Girl Scout "visit day" to get information and meet people. They ended up changing their minds, but I was glad that I let them go because they were telling me— literally—that they were ready to judge for themselves how faith and other ways of thinking worked in the Girl Scouts. At that point, they didn't quite like what they saw.

What about Community?

Now to be fair, we as humans are community-oriented animals. For the most part, we enjoy the company of others. Children are especially needy in this department. If you plan to avoid the advertising shenanigans of religious youth groups, what will you do to replace them? How will you help your child feel part of a larger group of people? Think hard on these questions because the answers have a great effect on how your child will ultimately judge your actions. It would be a tragedy to have your thoughtful considerations taken out of context.

For example, my girls were home when those two teenage sweethearts came to my door. In front of the children, I had to tell them no, thank you, we are not a religious family—twice, because they came back the next day. Afterward, we were honest with the children. We told them that going to church because they give you candy and play a game with you is not a good reason to go. We also told them all of the things we already do that are fun and enjoyable and that we would do those things according to our family's schedule (which they get to help decide). So what are some alternatives to religious camps and events?

School. First, realize that your children already participate in a community event Monday through Friday because they attend school. Take advantage of your child's schooling. Attend PTA meetings and other school events. Find that calendar that you usually throw away and plan to attend at least one event per month. Get to know the staff and some of the students in your child's classroom. Make an effort to go on one of the fieldtrips this year.

Donate and discuss. We've been donating since before our children were born. Once our children could put money in their hands, we had them donating to those less fortunate than themselves.

A community requires sacrifice for the betterment of all and giving in any form helps children recognize that. We donate to the Salvation Army bell ringers when we go to the store during the holidays every time we go to the store with our children. It makes them feel like they are helping others—and it only costs my family fifty cents. We donate clothes to homeless shelters. We donate books we no longer need. We donate food during food drives at school. I've donated blood and told the children about my contribution. If possible, try to donate in person; it feels different from clicking something online. Finally, you could work to create a donation day in your neighborhood so that it becomes an annual event.

Get active in your community. This is also an option, not just with donations of money or clothes but with donations of time. Many older youth can benefit from seeing individuals less fortunate than themselves by handing out food during the holidays (if you celebrate them) for an hour a week, helping to buy new toys for a sponsored child or family, or spending time at the local adult living community. Join the National Arbor Day Foundation and plant trees in the spring to help our planet produce the air we breathe. Have your child tutor younger, struggling students in school. It's important that children know this fact: Deeply religious people aren't the only people who help others.

Use community centers and community spaces. Nearly every community has a community center or something similar. They usually have a gym, sports activities, planned events, and many other things. Seek them out, allow your children to meet children that may not go to their school. Join these family fun centers and become a part of the community in which you live.

Experience different cultures. Children love the Chinese New Year festivals, the Cinco de Mayo festival, and all the rich celebrations of culture that our country embraces. Expose your children to these events. Go to the jazz festival, Irish fest, and local Kwanzaa celebrations. Discuss how they felt afterward. On vacations or getaways, search out the differences and highlight them. Difference isn't bad; it's wonderful.

Vote. Become a registered voter and know how your representatives are making the decisions that affect your area. Let your child become active in learning about the structures that create our laws. I tell my children that I vote because that's how I make sure people know what I think about things. I slowly teach them the voting process and the value of it. We read *Mama Went to Jail for the Vote* by Kathleen Karr. We talked about the tattered history of voting and what it means to make your voice heard in a democracy.

Online communities. Keep in mind, community doesn't have to be limited to the area in which we live. Online communities are used for evil so much that we as parents forget what a powerful tool for good they can be! Freethinking communities, forums, and chat spaces have begun to dot the landscape of America via the internet.

All over the country, freethinkers are connecting and the walls of isolation are breaking down. Can't find a freethinking community in your area? Be a pioneer—create one! What a cool gift to give your child: the gift of starting a community from the ground up!

Building a sense of community in your child's mind will take time, effort, and diligence on your part. It might start with joining the PTA and creating bonds with parents regardless of their faith. Perhaps you are the type of parent that will localize the freethinkers in your area and create ties with like-minded parents. Your family might decide to become a part of the Unitarian Church, which tends to welcome.

Whatever shape your outreach takes, it is well-worth the payoff. Children benefit so much from interacting with people in the diverse communities of our country; being "friends" with everyone in your community, no matter their differences, becomes a reality for young people instead of a goal. Ultimately, young people should know that a community is important and that community does *not* depend on religious faith alone.

8

O Christmas Tree: Holidays and Secularism

Children learn about the presence of holidays in our culture at a very young age, mainly through the passing down of traditional religious holiday celebrations—and this is a good thing. Not only does it help them understand the idea of shared traditions, it also builds understanding for diversity and culture. All this is true if children are properly introduced to tradition as a concept. The opposite side of shared traditions can fuel a dislike of others and the untrue notion that one faith is superior to all others. Take, for example, the children in my daughter's kindergarten class. They were children of Christ in no uncertain terms and for them the lines were drawn: Either you believed in God or you didn't. Either you were going to heaven or you would burn in hell. There was no in-between.

Alongside the fanaticism, American society has turned celebrating holidays into a money-driven enterprise. Children are targeted along with adults. There's no better time of year to turn off the television than between the months of November and December—and that is exactly what we tend to do in our home. The TV is plastered with happy boys and girls, their brightly colored toys taunting my children. It's tragic. What's worse is the moment one holiday is over, the advertisements for the next begin. One thing is certain: As a secular parent, you need to know that there is no place in the country that is insulated from the effects of faith-based holidays.

So if there is no escaping holiday celebration, what is a secular parent to do? First, it is important to recognize the fact that your child must know the truth behind holiday rituals. Rituals? That's right. We need to call religious holidays what they are: rituals that people participate in because it makes them feel closer to a shared God. That's not a bad thing. Most Americans have no idea of the history of holiday celebrations beyond what they are told as children—and that is a problem. For example, it is a fact that winter celebrations (consisting of largely the same things as Christmas) were celebrated long before the church decided to merge Christ's birthday with pagan celebrations.

When my children were school-aged and well-cemented in their critical thinking skills, I told them to venture into the religion section at the library and choose a book if they were interested. Then we could read and learn about that religion together. For the longest time, the children paid no attention to that request. Occasionally a book on some obscure faith would come into our house. We would read and chat about the tenets of the faith and, sometimes, imagine our lives in that situation. This is precious instructional time with your child that you cannot afford to miss out on.

Generally, my kids weren't interested in learning about other faiths, and I was OK with that. As long as they knew they could, I was happy. This may be the case with your family. The goal is to be religiously literate, not stuff religion down our children's throats. The religion section in any library or bookstore is a great place to start the conversation. Internet websites are also excellent sources. I do recommend that you spend your time researching and creating a list. Be sure to stick with the PBS-ish sites. These ".org" sites are designed to give information more than opinion. This is sure to give you and your family room to explore the ideas sans the coercion. The more you know about the rituals you participate in, the more you will be able to give your child a well-rounded view of faith.

After learning about the origins of major religious holidays, you must then decide (with your child's input, preferably) how much of an issue celebrating—or not celebrating—will be for your family. Basically, there are two paths you can travel when it comes to celebrating religious holidays: celebrating or abstaining, with various side roads along the way.

If you're a new convert to the secular parenting world, the two roads are even more cumbersome: Do you snatch holidays from your family or do you allow them to be celebrated? If you celebrate during the holiday season, how far will you take the celebration? We had never really celebrated Christmas before I moved to Missouri. As we became more cemented in the role of secular parents, choices needed to be made. Let's look a little closer at abstaining and celebrating before I discuss how our family deals with these holidays and our reasons for doing so.

Where's the Party? What Not Celebrating Looks Like

Just as there are many types of families, there are also many levels of involvement in any particular religious celebration. The first choice seems most obvious for a secular parent: abstaining or actively refusing to participate in all holidays. But there is also *selective celebration.* The idea behind this form of abstention is that for all the crap life throws at us as parents, there are things that we just can't or don't have the energy to combat. Who really cares if the school puts up a Christmas tree? A strict abstainer might, but a selective parent can look past such overreaches of faith. Selective celebrating usually involves separating the religious practice from the holiday tradition itself. But each of these deserves a bit more explanation.

If you choose to abstain in the strict sense of the word, you and your family will not participate in any religious events with any family members or friends either at school or family events or in your home. Your child will sit out these celebrations and you will deal with the consequences and conversations that follow. What are the advantages and disadvantages of not celebrating in this way?

A major advantage is that you rid your home of the rituals that may rob your children of their critical thinking skills. You also create an open, honest discussion of our country's rituals without the fear of "forsaking" God or any other supernatural being. You will also limit the confusion of celebrating something but not believing in it wholeheartedly. Take, for example, the following conversation:

Daughter: So, Dad, if Santa climbs down chimneys and we don't have a chimney, how will Santa get into our house?

Dad: Well, baby, he will come through the door.

Daughter: But, Dad, that's not what Santa does. He only comes down chimneys.

Dad: He'll make an exception for our house.

Daughter: Dad, how does Santa get to all the children in the world in one night?

Dad: Well, he only comes to the houses with good kids, like ours!

Daughter: So how good do you have to be for Santa to come? I've gotten in trouble lots of times this year. But I was good too. Will he still come to our house?

Dad: Yes.

Daughter: So you don't have to be perfectly good, just mostly good?

This conversation will continue until the dad snaps. He's got a most inquisitive daughter who is thinking about the inconsistencies between the real world and the story that she has been taught. She's flexing her critical thinking muscle. A child like this might be seen as pure torture to adults, but when they grow up, these children will be powerful members of society. Nothing will be taken at face value, problems will be approached from more than one angle, and logical fallacies will be stopped dead in their tracks.

Wouldn't it be nice if instead of creating irrational responses to his daughter, the child's father simply said, "Well, baby, it's a pretend story. Santa isn't real. We make him up so that Christmas is a more special time." Wouldn't that alleviate this poor child's frustrated mind? It would also keep the father from lying to his daughter to keep a story alive that is completely illogical.

Trust me, Santa isn't any less fun or amazing to kids when they learn he's pretend. When my daughters turned seven and eight, the status of Santa's existence became an issue. I simply said, "There are those who believe Santa is real, and there are those, like me, who think that some of the things Santa does makes him imaginary." Now, after an initial stir-up, my kids got the point. This led them to question the Tooth Fairy, the Easter Bunny, and all other "questionable" entities.

My husband and I came to the secular parenting world from the same point most secular parents start at: that of a former person of faith. Initially, we participated in the Santa Claus-Tooth Fairy fun. Our children were fed these things from the point of view of being real. Then came the explaining, the reality checks, and the guilt. I hated that I had lied to my children, but the pressures of family can compel you to if you aren't careful. On the other hand, if you have yet to expose your children (or if they aren't born yet), you'll be in a fantastic position to have fun with these traditions while at the same time differentiating between fact and fiction for your child. Some of us have a bit of backtracking to do!

Occasionally, my youngest will play devil's advocate. She'll declare, "Santa is real!" She smiles and laughs when she says it and I pretend to play along. "But how does he get down that small, dirty chimney?" I ask her. "How does he get to all those houses around the entire world in one night?" It's a cute game that lets me know she's not ready to give up Santa even though she's aware of his new status. More importantly, our girls know they will not be berated for their beliefs. They are free to believe, and I am free to question!

In addition to saving your child's critical thinking, abstaining from religious rituals gives you the opportunity to create your own family rituals. There are many families who have successfully thought of creative holidays that occur on or near the same date as religious ones. While many will mimic the holiday in every sense except the religious aspects, these "new traditions" stimulate a child's creativity, bond families together, and keep children from feeling a sense of loss.

We've looked at a couple of advantages. So what are the disadvantages of completely abstaining from holiday traditions? The most obvious will be a feeling of isolation. Imagine being the only sister or brother in your family to not come to Hanukah celebrations or Easter Sunday mass. Missing the big family dinner on Christmas can sure leave scars on your relationship with extended family. It may seem easy for you as a parent, but I guarantee your child will notice the separateness—and feel the tension among adults who think that what you are doing is wrong.

A sad but true example of this can be found in a little boy we'll call Eric. Eric was four. Eric's father was a Muslim with the Nation of Islam. He could not afford to send his son to a private Muslim school. His only alternative was to send his son to a regular daycare, which just so happened to be my first job. Eric's father had made his position on the celebration of religious holidays clear: no singing of Christmas songs, no playing games that had to do with Christmas, no touching the Christmas tree—nothing. Eric was isolated in a world of what seemed to be happiness. We as a staff were not allowed to give him any of the cookies shaped like trees or bells. He couldn't have candy canes. He generally spent his days frustrated and playing alone.

I get where Eric's dad was coming from. He didn't want his kid to participate in holiday traditions that were not his own. What he failed to consider was what kind of world that left his son in for an extended period of time. All day, Monday through Friday, Eric was tormented by things he wanted to do but was forbidden by his father. I do remember him eventually eating cookies, but in general the month of December was awful for him—and for us. We desperately wanted to make him feel happy. Some suggested a neutral approach to celebrating, but the owner of the center was adamant. She was a Christian and she would be having the daycare center celebrate Christmas.

My time with Eric taught me that I needed to be realistic in my parenting as well. How could I expect my child to endure something like that day in and day out? We know that children are social beings; they need to feel connected to their peer group.

As parents, we should consider the limitations of our environment. At times, a completely secular lifestyle just might not be possible. A bigger question, however, on totally abstaining from holiday celebrations should float to the surface here: Is all of this worth your child's frustration?[18]

Eric's story isn't limited to childcare. It can be a huge emotional strain on your child if their school is choosing to break the separation of church and state doctrine. I've dedicated a chapter to this because it really needs to be flushed out. If you are dealing with a private child care system, you are pretty much at the whim of the owners, and if this is your only form of childcare, then making life miserable for your child simply isn't the way to go. There should never be an Eric in the room.

In these situations it is all too common that teachers and other professionals will also try to undermine your wishes. There were plenty of times that I heard someone say to Eric, "It's OK if you do that. I won't tell your dad." Eventually, Eric gave in. What was he supposed to? Sit in a corner feeling bad while all his friends had a

---

[18]If your child is under age eight, then my answer to this question is yes. Organized religion is dangerous for children who have not yet developed the critical thinking skills to figure out what they are participating in and if they agree with the tenets, but there are ways to save the family connectedness that we all love while not compromising your principals on religion.

great time? The sad thing is the relationship between Eric and his father has been forever changed.

What you must determine as a secular parent is how your children will react to any abrupt changes in lifestyle, if they can successfully adjust to those changes, and if those changes were worth the frustration and disruption in the long run. There are certainly more advantages and disadvantages to not celebrating religious holidays. But before deciding to abstain, consider stretching your thinking to include the opposite side. What are the advantages and disadvantages of celebrating religious holidays?

Celebration Station: What Can Happen on This Road?

Holiday traditions and secular parenting would seem, initially at least, to be diametrically opposed. My hope is that a quick story might shed some light on a secular parenting decision to practice any degree of holiday celebration.

When I decided to move my family from Seattle to Kansas City, a level of hope and excitement surged in me: I was twenty-four and leaving the only place I'd ever called home to start a new life in the Midwest—and my two small children were coming with me. We traveled by train from Seattle, through Oregon, and down to Los Angeles. Then we boarded a different train and spent another two days working our way toward the small town of Kirksville, Missouri, where we settled.

But while the cities I saw were spectacular and the people were generally kind, a sense of fear began to swell inside of me. We would be alone in Kirksville, a tiny, new family with no friends and a lot of responsibility. I was to start college, the children needed daycare, and we had zero funds other than my "school money."

By the time the train pulled into the La Plata station ten miles from Kirksville, the fear of isolation had grown into a near panic attack. What had I done? Could I undo it if I needed to? And as we came around the corner and opened the door to our new, mostly unfurnished house, I simply wanted to see my husband's smile. But he was at work—I knew he would be. Instead of seeing his bright green eyes, we rounded the corner and saw a three-and-half foot tall, fully decorated Christmas tree. It was plugged in, and as the lights bounced off the walls, off the boxes full of our shipped life, and off the ceiling, everything felt suddenly right.

That was the first "Christmas tree" my children ever saw, and the way they fell over themselves trying to reach it and the collective "wow" that came from their mouths was something I will always remember. That tree mattered to me. It mattered that my husband had taken the time to put up a perfect tree, a tree that represented the start of our new family. What didn't matter to me, what wasn't even a passing thought, was the fact that the Christmas tree itself was associated with Christ.

Having shared traditions creates a sense of shared identity, a type of closeness that makes one feel whole. To this day, the only time many families get together is during the holidays. If you choose to celebrate any holiday, a sense of community will be your biggest gain. There's no denying it: One thing religion does do is create a common thread in families, towns, and cities. A shared set of values means that when your child goes to school, to grandma's house, or to a neighborhood party, they will have a commonality that bonds them to those individuals.

Another advantage of celebrating holiday traditions, and probably the best for you as a parent, is a lack of stress and concern over holiday events. When we go to a family member's house for Thanksgiving, I know for a fact that the issue of prayer will come up. Someone will say that it is "so sad what she's doin' with those kids." How is that not a fight-starter? The issue, however, disappears if you give in to holiday traditions. If your child celebrates all holidays, then there's no need to protest the Christmas tree at school, no need to talk to family members about your reasons and rationale for not celebrating. Basically, it's the easy way out of a tough situation.

A major disadvantage of celebrating holidays is that your child's critical thinking may suffer. Sure, Jesus could have been born of a virgin, even though we know that people physically must have some sort of "contact." Logic can be easily dissolved with one quick phrase: "Well, that's what I believe." Recall our earlier reading of the father and daughter? You may find yourself in this boat. To that effect, you become a perpetual liar if you don't acknowledge what we know to be true about life and our experiences as human beings— based, of course, on facts. Once your child reaches the age of reason, your child comes to believe two things: 1) All parents unabashedly lie to their children about some things, and 2) lying to children is OK in some situations.

Perhaps the most concrete of frustrations comes in the form of guilt. We as parents already fear of ruining the children that we are so fortunate to have. This makes guilt a strong determiner in our actions. I've had people tell me I'm a horrible mother for telling the truth about Santa, the Easter Bunny, and God. "You're taking away the fun of childhood!" they say. "You've ruined something you were allowed to have." At times, I would wonder if I was making a mistake. Was it fair to put the pressure of faith on my child?

And if you're thinking or feeling any of that right now, I want you to listen up and listen well. This world placed the weight of religion on the shoulders of your children the moment they were born. Our job as parents is not to hide the challenge of faith, but to explain it. Children are no less excited about Christmas because they know family and friends are buying them gifts instead of an imaginary chubby guy in a red and white suit. Christmas is bigger than Santa, and if you open your child up to this perspective, I believe any guilt you have will subside.

The truth is that celebrating holiday traditions as a secular family blurs the lines between tradition and fact. Since the central tenets of secular parenting are knowledge acquisition, honesty, and freedom of choice, we must keep the truth at the forefront of our intentions as parents. *Remember: Because something is a tradition doesn't mean it's true.* It's simply what has always been done. If you always throw salt over your shoulder when you walk under a bridge, that doesn't mean the bridge will collapse if you forget your salt shaker next time. If children celebrate religious traditions as if they are true, there is bound to be some conversations about how some things just don't seem to make sense. What will happen when your child asks if Santa really visits all children? Or if they can eat just a little during the day for Ramadan and not be punished by Allah? How you teach your child the difference between religious tradition and fact when celebrating those traditions sends clear messages, whether you intend them to or not.

The Best of Both Worlds

Our family chose to loosely celebrate holidays, mostly because we became nonreligious after our children began celebrating holidays. We didn't want our children to experience the sense of loss that many children report after being ripped from familiar traditions. In addition to loss, there is anger and contempt. That seethes in a child. I didn't want my girls to look back and see my actions as a punishment in any way. Our goal as parents is to create freethinking children, and we felt abrupt separation for some of our children's most beloved events would drive a wedge in that goal. Diehard secularists will disagree. That's OK: Not every secular parent is alike; we have degrees of tolerance.

My husband and I also felt very strongly that children should know the religious foundations of holidays, what they mean, and why we do not celebrate them in a more ritualistic way. As I said before, you and your family must research Hanukah, Ramadan, Christmas or whatever tradition is present in your children's lives. It is important to explain to them—as objectively as possible—the fact versus tradition each ritual presents.

The conversations we had with our children took place over several days, mostly near the holiday itself. Overloading children is common in secular homes, so you will want to keep your conversations short (especially for the very young) so they can think about what they have learned. We kept our conversations to less than five minutes. This was just enough time to get the facts out, answer (or pose) a question or two, and send them off to play! Any longer and you risk a child simply shutting down or forgetting the point.

Several conversations on the subject of holidays would follow. We began by asking our children if they liked celebrating Christmas and why. Of course, we got the usual response: "It's fun to get presents. It's nice to see family." We then moved to a conversation about the religious foundations of Christmas according to Christian mythology. It was so exciting to hear an eight-year-old discuss the merits of things like the Ten Commandments and the resurrection of Christ. Not once had I been given such an opportunity at their age!

During our next chat, we moved past religion and looked deeper at the ritual itself. We talked about the history of Christmas and how Christmas celebrations predate the supposed birth of Christ. We kept these conversations going, in small bits, throughout the Christmas season. Our children still enjoyed presents, family, and friends, but, more importantly, they also had a balanced view of a holiday of which many children only get to hear one side. We were building a foundation of a knowledge one religious chunk at a time.

We also discussed the birth and resurrection mythology when spring's pretty colors brought up the Easter Bunny. We talked about the realistic aspects of the holiday (how this was supposed to be the burial and resurrection of Jesus). Jesus was born from a virgin, he died because the rulers thought he was bad, and during that time they punished bad people by nailing them to a cross.

We also talked about the parts that defy logic and reality—a man rising from the grave (after being interred in a tomb with the entrance covered by an enormous stone) and ascending to heaven (a place for which we have no solid proof of existence). We asked the children what they thought of the story and had a few clarifying conversations. Again, this was not done all at once. That is simply too much for little ones to take in!

One important aspect of our conversation centered on those who believe the resurrection mythology. Our children were told some people take it literally and so even though it may sound silly to them—they laughed at the idea of someone floating through the sky—it's serious to others. I tell them it's their choice to believe in that or not, but that is not why we celebrate Easter—we do it for the chocolate!

But seriously, we have found that denying our children the right to participate in a cultural norm, particularly one the majority of their friends celebrate, could have damaging and counterproductive effects. We felt it better (and our duty) to balance what they get in the outside world with knowledge about a ritual's history and our reasons for believing or disbelieving the mythology. This way, children can truly make up their minds given both perspectives of the situation.

Does this mean that everything done by others in a society must be celebrated? Of course not. As parents, we pick and choose our battles. We laid down the law when it came to rituals like eating the body of Christ in church and worshipping through prayer, but most aspects of traditional holidays we celebrated.

For a secular parent, trusting your child to decide whether or not Jesus was resurrected can be a little frustrating. Some kids still don't know how to tie their shoes at age seven. How can we expect them to have an idea of or to start a conversation about God? This is a moot point. *We can trust the system of educating, exposing, and discussing.* This type of trust requires that we remember children are individuals, not replicas of their parents. Our job is to allow a well-rounded choice to take place. Raising a secular child does not guarantee that they will be a secular adult. That is not the point. The point of raising secular children is to give them the opportunity to truly choose what it is they think of the various viewpoints represented by the world's religions. Raising a secular child ensures that they have a deep respect for life, diversity, and what it means to be a productive member of a society where *everyone* matters, not just those in their flock.

Is This Hypocrisy?

Should I vow to never eat an Easter egg, never buy a bow in the month of December, and never light any candles for Hanukah? Not only is that a bit extreme, it's not realistic. Hypocrisy is denouncing something and then doing what you denounced. As an atheist, I do not believe in God, heaven, or hell. My reasons for participating in Christian holidays have nothing to do with God, heaven, or hell. I have purposely pulled the religion out of the tradition and for my family that works. I live in a culture that celebrates said holidays and beliefs, and I choose to allow my children to participate—at a distance. During no point in the celebrating of holidays do I invoke the God, heaven, hell, or any other religiousness, yet my children are aware of the holiday's religious origin.

As a teacher, I get two weeks off for Christmas, and since I don't see my family often, I use that time to my advantage. They all celebrate Christmas, most know that we are atheists, and despite this we have a lovely time together. I respect my family's right to prayer, and they respect my decision to not participate.[19]

---

[19]In addition to celebrating or not celebrating religious holidays, there are several holidays centered around secular (or humanistic) principals. I found this nifty website for learning more about secular holiday traditions: http://secularseasons.org/celebrations/ seasons.html.

Ultimately, you have to decide which holiday road you and your family should travel. To help you decide, ask yourself the following questions

How important is this holiday, really, to my family?

Can I alter this holiday to create a family tradition of our own to replace the religious traditions associated with the holiday?

Have I told my family and friends about my views on this particular holiday? Will they respect my wishes?

Have I given my child a more objective, practical view of this holiday to balance what they will encounter in the world?

Every family is different and what works for one may not be appropriate for another. By answering the above questions, you will be on the right track to making an informed decision.

Tradition versus Fact:
Does Your Child Know the Difference?

It makes sense to end this chapter with a quick conversation about tradition versus fact and ensuring that children understand the difference. One of my earliest memories is watching my grandmother make cornbread. Her mechanical movements and unchanging logic mesmerized me every time I would visit. The conversations we would have are perfect openers for understanding tradition and comparing them to facts. I was about seven when I first started helping my grandma make cornbread and the conversations would go something like this:

Me: Grandma, how come you don't use the cornbread mix? It's easier.

Grandma: Cornbread mix! What are you talkin' 'bout? You don't make cornbread with no mix! Here, first you get the flour and the cornmeal . . .

Me: Grandma, why do you put so much butter in your cornbread? Butter is bad for you. You are supposed to use margarine.

Grandma: Margarine! I ain't never used margarine a day in my life! You make cornbread with butter. Butter and oil. That's how my momma made it and her momma too.

. . . And it would continue. My grandma knew tradition. She was born and raised on a farm in Shreveport, Louisiana. She moved north in the late 40s to have and raise her children, but she was a southern girl until the day she died. She had so many things that she did because "that's how it was supposed to be done." There were certain ways to make cornbread, rice pudding, and all kinds of food. Grandma had sayings that made no sense to me: *She didn't have a pot to piss in or a window to throw it out of!* It was hard to understand her sometimes. I knew she loved me, but she was from another planet.

I, on the other hand, am a product of the 80s. Born into a time when scientific advancements dominated our world on many fronts, my generation was filled with the internet, healthy eating, computers, and the rights of all Americans to be treated equally. My grandmother was a link to a time before I existed and she had little desire to see the world at any other point in time. She never used a computer, never drove a car, and never cooked with anything but pure butter. She'd been around when Dr. Martin Luther King, Jr., and JFK were alive, and she even remembered having to use bathrooms that said "Colored" on the door. With my grandma, I could learn about my family's way of dealing with tradition and life in America.

Of course, none of this speaks to the validity of my grandma's actions. Because my grandma refused to use Jiffy Cornbread Mix did not mean that her cornbread was better. And just because my grandma refused—quite literally—to diet, exercise, or eat foods that were from other cultures doesn't mean that dieting, exercise, or trying new foods are bad things.

You and I can see this as adults, but to a child, the line between fact and tradition is quite blurry. After almost thirty years, I still make cornbread from scratch. I have the recipe in my head, I rarely measure—thanks, Grandma—and for some reason, I have begun instructing my seven-year-old in the art of proper cornbread making.

If we transfer the same unbending, traditional attitude to children, one can see how a problem might arise. Many of the things done in religion are done to preserve the rituals or traditions of the faith: We eat the body and drink the blood of Christ purely because that's what has always been done (surely none of us actually think cannibal-like behavior is the right thing to do). We attend church, the mosque, and other houses of worship because that's the traditional way of showing devotion to our religion. Doing these things does not mean that they are right or wrong.

How do we teach our children the difference between tradition and fact? **First, children need a working definition of tradition and tradition's limitations.** You know your child best, so the level of conversation will be yours to determine. I told our children that

Tradition is doing something because that's the way your mom or grandma did it, talking a certain way because that's how it's always been said, or thinking certain ways about things because that's how it's always been looked at.

Because I like to do something a certain way doesn't mean it's right. I gave the example of putting raisins in my oatmeal. I hate oatmeal without raisins, but that doesn't mean that oatmeal without raisins is wrong or bad. It's just not what I would do.

Traditions (like making cornbread with Grandma) can be fun and harmless.

Just because a way of thinking—such as religion—is very old doesn't mean it's true. For example, it used to be thought that taking vitamin C before or during a cold would help it go away faster. A recent finding proves that in most cases, while vitamin C does many things for our body, getting rid of a cold is not one of them.

We need to ask ourselves what can happen when a group of people think that a tradition is true. What would happen if people actually believed "if you step on a crack, you break your mama's back"?

Next, children should have examples of traditions to analyze. I've talked with my children about some things that used to be "just how things were always done."

When our country was first created, white people made black people slaves and most people thought it was OK. What do you think about that?

When Grandma was little, women didn't have the right to vote because most men thought women weren't able to understand politics. Do you think women can do that?

Most people in our country right now think that women and men are the only people who should get married. Do you think a man and a man or a woman and a woman should be allowed to get married if they love each other?

Finally, teach your child to spot the facts in any given situation. How do we know that women are or are not able to understand politics like men? A fact is something that can be proven objectively. Critical thinking can help us determine if something is indeed a statement of fact or just an opinion. Spotting these differences only get easier with practice. Walking down the street, driving on the way to school, sitting at the dinner table—all of these are great places to bring up questions and ask your child, "Is it a fact or an opinion?"

In the end, the balancing of tradition and fact is something your children will do their entire lives. Even now, new traditions for your children to analyze are popping up and old traditions are fading into antiquity. How will your children realize the fun or folly in a tradition if they are not taught that there is indeed a difference?

9

The Chat 2.0: Time to Update

For the girls!

"Now I lay me down to sleep,

I pray the Lord my shape to keep.

Please no wrinkles, please no bags,

and please lift my butt before it sags.

Please no age spots, please no gray,

and as for my belly, please take it away.

Please keep me healthy, please keep me young,

and thank you, dear Lord, for all that you've done."

—Internet Forward

One of the early editors of my book read this chapter and said "I think it strikes the wrong tone. Publishers want something with broader appeal." An editor of an even earlier version suggested that I be a bit more sensitive to parents and publishers when it comes to talking about sex and children. But the truth is that this chapter, above any other, requires honesty—brutal, cruel, anger-provoking honesty. Our kids are being crippled by their sexual decisions while at the same time they are bombarded with sex on a daily basis. We don't have time to talk nice here. So this chapter begins right where it should: with a sad little internet forward.

The moment I saw the poem above, like any parent, my heart sank. It took me back to my own body-image years: middle school. That's when I met my first boy-bully. We'll call him John. Every day for most of the school year, John reminded me that my breasts were "uneven." What a nice guy, right? I would try to avoid John, but assigned seats mandated that I sat near him. I hated John. I would go home and stare at my breasts in the mirror for hours, begging God to fix them . . . and my hairy legs . . . and the dark circles around my eyes . . . and my brown skin . . . and—

The fact is that all adolescents are insecure about their bodies, and I can bet that you were no different at that age. We can't get rid of the Johns of the world, but through conversations about sex, bodies, and healthy relationships, they cease to leave such a painful mark. If, for example, I'd known that breasts often grow at different rates, I would have only felt like John was a jerk. Instead, I also felt like I'd been given a broken body. I needed a "sex talk" badly. But all I really got was "sex is overrated" and "don't get pregnant." Enlightening, right?

Of course, my parents are not alone. As a result of our "sex talk"-issues in America, even the most academic among us have lost the ability to effectively communicate on the subject of sex. In my junior year of college, I took a literature for young adults class—a requirement for English majors. There sat next to me some of the brightest young adults in the Midwest. One of the topics we studied was youth, sexuality, and young adult literature. Words like penis, orgasm, and masturbation inevitably came up. Over half of the class flat-out refused to speak—even when prompted by the professor. Eventually the conversation was just between the professor and a few students. One of the women in the class raised her hand and said, "These words and this conversation is uncomfortable for me. I don't want to talk about this anymore." My question to this twenty-two-year-old woman is the same question I want to begin this chapter with:

If we as adults cannot discuss sex, bodies, and sexuality, how can we help our children make sexually responsible choices?

Suddenly my irritation that day in class gave way to an explosion of anger that became difficult to contain. I was almost irate. We weren't in high school. We were supposed to be the nation's thinkers;

we were men and women of words and in that class of adults, the mere mention of ordinary body parts was off limits.

And that's why the frustration that I felt about my breasts all those years ago is no different from the frustration your child will most likely experience at some point. Unfortunately, our tendency as parents is to respond to "body problems" the way our parents did, and if we don't change that, our children will suffer. It isn't the 1970s or 80s—it's isn't even the 19-anythings anymore. Our world is no longer as simple. Let us consider some of the ways that "adults" have dealt with the topic of sex and sexuality in this country of late:

Pornography is a multi-billion dollar industry that, thanks to the World Wide Web, is available to children and adults twenty four hours a day.

Religious fundamentalism, in an attempt to deal with promiscuous youth, has created "hell houses" to scare young adults into sexually compliant roles and behaviors—regardless of the mental or physical consequences.

Rap and other pop culture videos, which are mostly watched by children ages six and up, enforce sexuality as a means of obtaining power, control, and wealth. These videos amount to soft, cable-sponsored pornography.

Nearly all forms of advertisement in the U.S.—food, hygiene, movies, cars and, in some cases, employment opportunities—use sex or sexuality to sell their ideas, products and services.

The Disney Channel and other "children's channels" regularly promote adult clothing, mannerisms, and sexual undertones in their programming for children ages eight and up.

Teachers, principals, and parents have begun disbanding after-school groups because of their contempt for gay, lesbian, bi-sexual and transgender students who wish to form support systems at school.

Though it is a fact that children of all ages masturbate, children are still spanked, hit, and berated for touching their bodies in a sexually expressive way.

Many parents were taught (and still teach their own children) that masturbation is at the very least wrong and at worst can endanger your mortal soul.

Children under the age of thirteen are being arrested and jailed for sexual assault on other children as young as six years old.

Most adults can barely say penis, vagina, or breasts without laughing, wiggling or pretending to completely disappear.

Indeed, our relationship with sex has become distorted, abusive, and generally unhealthy. In schools, for example, where children spend most of their waking hours, teachers are afraid to broach the subject of sex for fear of lawsuits. At home, parents talk too little, don't really answer questions, or simply hope their children will make it through adolescence without becoming a teen parent or dying of AIDS. All the while, our young ones get mixed or flat-out wrong messages and often have no clear idea on what to do when they feel the natural urges that surround the adolescent years.

It makes sense, then, that parents sometimes turn to fear tactics and eternal damnation for the answers to raising sexually responsible children. What else can we do? My sex talk occurred at the age of thirteen—long after my friends had filled my brain with nonsense. I was sitting in the living room nursing a bad headache. I told my mom about it. Her response would consist of two sentences: 1) Sex is overrated. 2) Don't get pregnant. What on earth am I supposed to do with that at the age of thirteen?

Now I am a mother of two daughters. As they grow, my own fears about their future choices continues to grow. My first thought was to build a wall around them until they were at least twenty-five (my husband thought that was a wonderful idea), but pretending like sex can't happen to our children will not teach them how react when they're confronted with it. Neither will pretending sex doesn't exist teach girls how to be aware of their surroundings, their drinks, or the people they meet at parties. It also won't teach boys that "no means no," even when they've been allowed to kiss, rub, and pull down pants. It might sound terrible to think about, but these are just a few of the *real* skills a young adult needs today.

This kind of teaching—realistic teaching—will help prevent unwanted sexual advances, venereal diseases, and teenage parents. A wall, as nice as it sounds, will only separate your child from a society in which they will soon be a part. A wall will only stop them from experiencing natural sexual attraction and create repressed feelings that will need to be vented at some point—most likely after a poor sexual decision. So what options are there for helping young people make sexually responsible choices?

Let's start with the facts.

Abstinence-Only Education:
What Do the Facts Say?

Americans have already tried to build that wall. We've decided against the idea of honesty and communication with our young adults—it's much easier to focus on what we *want* as parents instead of what they *need* as maturing sexual beings.

It helps here if we review a bit of history. With Roe v. Wade legalizing abortion and the birth control pill in full swing by the 1970s, many in America felt we were going down the wrong path of sexual "freedom." Enter the birth of the evangelical right and the Adolescent Family Life Act of 1982. On the surface, it does seem like a good idea: Teach kids that saving themselves for marriage is a great thing, a worthwhile thing—the only thing to do. The goal was to stop the flood of STIs, pregnancies, and the other negative consequences of sex that all parents want to erase. But that was in 1982, and the facts of today show a much needed reform of the Family Life Act. When Marty Klein wrote *America's War on Sex*, he basically summed up the findings on the subject:

> Abstinence only programs don't protect kids from disease, pregnancy, or broken hearts. That's because they aren't effective at postponing sexual involvement or at making kids safer when they do have sex. . . . So abstinence programs don't help kids. But they do benefit adults—both emotionally and financially. Abstinence programs help [adults] convince themselves that kids are less sexual than they really are. They get to maintain the illusion that kids aren't doing it, are going to stop doing it, or aren't going to start.

Klein hit it right on the money with this quote. It might make us feel better knowing our children are being taught to only think of marriage. Many of us still believe in that old "out of sight, out of mind" adage. But it's a scary kind of logic. The argument "Because my child doesn't know about condom use, birth control, or STI's, they won't be sexual" simply doesn't hold water.

Furthermore, the facts don't lie. In 2001, the National Campaign to Prevent Teen Pregnancy published a review called "Emerging

Answers: Research Findings on Programs to Reduce Teen Pregnancy." It concluded that "the evidence is not conclusive about the impact of abstinence-only programs" and that "there do not currently exist any abstinence-only programs with reasonably strong evidence that they actually delay the initiation of sex or reduce its frequency." The review, however, did little to stop the stampede of school districts—desperate for help—that latched on to the failing abstinence-only program.

Finally, in 2005, the *Journal of Adolescent Health* found that teens who pledge abstinence until marriage are more likely to have oral and anal sex than other teens who have not had intercourse. In 2007, a long awaited, federally-mandated study that began in 1997 concluded that abstinence-only programs do not keep teenagers from having sex. Neither do such programs increase or decrease the likelihood that, if they do have sex, teenagers will use condoms.

Of late, many states have either begun to reject federal funding for abstinence-only programs or have created hybrid versions that allow for full sex education (discussions of condom use, birth control, and pregnancy options) while still stressing abstinence. I like this approach, but the hybrid-programs aren't coming fast enough.

If your child's school district is using abstinence-only programs to teach sex and sexuality, beware! It's important that you ask to see what's being taught, and, more importantly, how that education program addresses the mental and physical aspects of sex, situation dynamics (such as what to do if you don't want to have sex but your boyfriend won't let up), birth control, and pre-marital sex. There are many programs that flat-out lie to teens. I once had a girl tell me that she learned—*learned!*—that sex before marriage is psychologically damaging. That's categorically untrue. If you're twenty-two years old, sexually responsible, and in a committed relationship, there is nothing wrong with having sex. This strict way of thinking is imposed on society by religious claims that God demands celibacy until marriage. And while, yes, waiting until you are with a partner who values who you are is the goal, abstinence-only programs oftentimes do not lean in this direction—and I believe that our children need to be prepared for both realities.

My main issue with abstinence-only programs is that they create a very narrow viewpoint of sex and sexuality. They demonize the act of sex and use the fear of disease and social stigma to scare teens into not "doing it." The end result is a horny yet guilt-ridden teenager who has no one to turn to for solution-based advice and in turn makes poor sexual decisions.

Real Sex Education:
A Holistic Approach to a Natural Phenomenon

The answer to the question of teaching young adults to make healthy, sexually responsible choices lies in using society, both its positives and negatives, to produce a sexually-competent child. Remember, ignorance does not equal innocence. Ignorance equals a child who is unprepared to live in society and who will be taken advantage of. If you believe never discussing sex, abstinence, condoms, vaginas, penises, or masturbation will keep your child from making sexual decisions, then you will create just what you are trying to prevent: a sexually-irresponsible child. As secular parents, we must approach sex and sexuality head-on. But first we need to prepare ourselves. Below are five very important messages that will serve to ground both you as a parent and your child as a future sexual being.

Have a reality check. What is your sexual comfort level? Our parents and our childhood experiences play a huge role in how we view sex. If you had very sexually open parents, then this chapter will be more of a nice review for you. Most of us, however, had parents who were shackled to old ways and religious fear. Remember my big sex talk? This was significantly better than my husband's "big talk." As I've mentioned, his father was a Baptist preacher. There was never any mention of sex in my husband's childhood. It was simply understood that sex and bodies were sinful. A friend of mine, as early as age two, was made to bathe without his mother in the bathroom—

in a tub full of water!—because it was improper for women (including his mother) to look at him. Before you speak to your child about sex, engrain these truisms into your head:

- Sex is a natural, beautiful expression of love between two consenting individuals.

- There is nothing nasty, dirty, or wrong with using the anatomically correct names for the parts of the body when speaking to children. Why use anything else?

- Sex is more than a physical act. It is an emotional investment with mental and physical consequences.

- Masturbation is a healthy and natural way to please oneself and is a great alternative to sex for young adults.

You may need convincing after that last one! Truly, though, masturbation is the safest alternative to sex without hurting one's mental or physical health—more on that later. Keeping these five things in mind will help you change your outlook on sex and sexual behavior, specifically if you were taught how evil and wrong these things were.

You really are your child's only hope here. It is imperative that you provide a holistic approach to sex. If sex is an uncomfortable subject for you, re-read the bulleted statements above and post them somewhere you will see them often. Are those statements not enough? I can accept that, but you are still on the hook for your child's sexual awareness so grab a book on talking with kids about sex—there are millions of them out there!

I am tempted to add here that, if you still find it difficult to talk with your child about sex, you should find someone who will—but I won't. I have found that, without a doubt, you are the biggest influence on your child's sexuality. Sure, you cannot control their sexuality. But what you can control is the degree to which you make your child aware of the consequences, good and bad, associated with sex and sexual experiences. What would it say to your children about the nature of sex, sexuality, and the body if you couldn't even talk about it with them? What happens when they're having a sexual crisis and they need guidance—like, "If I don't sleep with him, he'll break up with me," or, "If I don't sleep with her, all my friends will say I'm gay"? You absolutely must find it in yourself to look beyond your anxieties and be the role model you signed on to be. Counseling, talking with your partner or spouse, and journaling are all good options for overcoming your negative relationship with sex, if one exists.

One last thought on this. When my husband and I first began our sex conversations (because you will need more than one), my husband didn't really say anything. I did most of the talking. But he was *there*. It matters that both parents take a vested interest in letting their child know the beauty and the dangers surrounding sex.

Always use the correct names for parts of the body with your child. The positive effects of using the anatomically correct names for body parts have been extremely well researched and documented. The findings suggest that not only does it promote a healthy body image, it also helps young children identify with absolute certainty whether or not they have been inappropriately touched by an adult. Law enforcement agencies, psychologists that interview children, and many national organizations for young children will readily agree that the proper names for body parts are best. This language should be used from the time a child can sing, "Head and shoulders, knees and toes." The American Academy of Pediatrics lays out helpful guidelines for when a child begins to ask questions about sex and body parts. They say,

- Don't laugh or giggle, even if the question is cute. Your child may feel ashamed for her curiosity.

- Be brief. Don't go into a long explanation. Answer in simple terms. Your four-year old doesn't need to know the details of intercourse.

- Be honest. Use proper names for all body parts.

- See if your child wants or needs to know more. Follow up your answers with "Does that answer your question?"

- Listen to your child's responses and reactions.

- Be prepared to repeat yourself.

If you are uneasy talking about sex or answering certain questions, be honest about that too. It can be very uncomfortable for parents who are not used to using "the words" at first. Letting your child know this will help ease the tension and let them realize that you are trying to give the best advice.

Trust me, if you give it time, "penis," "breasts," and "vagina" will be names of body parts (as they should be) and nothing more. Having worked in many NAEYC[20]-accredited daycares, I had no problem saying to one of my daughters one day to "watch out for Daddy's penis. You don't want to kick it with your foot." My husband, on the other hand, was quite uncomfortable until, as a family, we became desensitized to those words—though as our girls got older, their sensitivity returned and they chose to use them less frequently.

Educate your children. Educate yourself. I would be lying to you if I tried to pretend like all the sexual education you needed was in this book. Once, my five-year-old came home from kindergarten and said, "Mom, what does 'sexy' mean? Michael said I looked 'sexy' today in gym." I knew then that we needed to really begin sex education—which meant I needed to do some research. First, I

---

[20]National Association for the Education of Young Children

bought the infamous *Where Did I Come From?* book. Remember what I said earlier about your sexual comfort level? This book will really challenge it! It was written by a couple of parents in the 70s who were tired of all the ridiculous ways people were explaining sex to young children.

After we bought the book, my husband and I kept it in our room for a few weeks. We actually laughed and giggled at the naked cartoon images and the weird ways the authors tried to explain orgasms. We read it, discussed it, read it again, decided what we'd say to the children, role-played questions and responses, and then set a date to read it with them. We might have taken it a *bit* seriously. We read that book as a family, all four of us on the couch. My husband didn't speak the entire time, but he was there.

One of my daughters, the oldest, was obviously interested and embarrassed at the same time. Her curiosity told me that it was a good idea, and her embarrassment said that I would need to tread slowly and lightly. The younger just laughed, tried to copy the longer words and new phrases I was saying, and generally had a good time. I was careful to clarify and talk about our family view of sex, relationships, and bodies (we'll talk about that more in a minute). When we finished, I told the girls I'd leave the book on the table for them to look at whenever they wanted.

When we left the room, that book was in a child's hands. The crazy thing is that I was proud of this; I wanted my children to learn about sex the right way. If that meant that they wanted to do it in my absence, so be it. To be fair, the book has its shortcomings. It doesn't really discuss female pleasure at all, and it's a bit dated. But it is a great start for younger children. We have added to our collection with *The Period Book* by Karen Gravelle and a few others. *What's Going on Down There?* is great for boys by Gravelle as well.

This is an area where reaching out to organizations with structured programs is a good idea as well. Most Unitarian Universalist Churches offer sex education classes that are spectacular, including discussions on sex, healthy relationships, abstinence, and birth control. Local Planned Parenthoods or other community centers will have strong programs as well. These are vital resources that should not be overlooked.

With abstinence-only programs replacing actual sexual education in many areas, you must take the responsibility for creating a sexually healthy child in your own hands. Empowering children with knowledge is key. The reality is that abstinence is truly the best and healthiest choice for young adults. We should stress this. But we also should use common sense here—we know that young people don't always do what's best for them.

Create and share your family values about sex with your child. I use every opportunity that presents itself to tell my children what I think about sex, sexual behaviors, and the consequences of those behaviors. My goal is not to be overbearing but consistent.

This has lessened as they've aged, and I'm sure the same will be true for you. My thoughts are not grounded in a desire to scare or control my child's sexual behavior. Rather, my feelings are grounded in the hope of creating a productive member of society who can interact with the opposite sex in a healthy manner. I tell my children

Sex is not bad, but having sex before your body is mature will hurt your body and the way you think about things.

Sex is a special thing. You should only have sex with someone who is very special and who loves you very much. That is why it is best to wait until you are older and committed (preferably in a serious relationship or married).

When you have sex before your body is ready, it can change the way your mind thinks about men and women. (Here we talk about things like thinking that sex will make a boy or a girl love you and the dangerous activities that can result from using sex to get affection.)

If you become pregnant or get someone pregnant before you've gone to   college and found a job, it will be harder to take care of yourself *and* your baby.

It is better to wait until you can take care of a child—that is, it is better to wait until you've decided what you want to do for work and found a partner who loves you before you have sex.

There are lots of things you can do with your boyfriend or girlfriend instead of having sex to feel close.

There are infections—such as viruses and bacteria—that you can catch while having sex that can hurt your body and make it hard to have children when you are ready. This is why you must choose your partner wisely.

There are lots of ways to show you love someone instead of having sex with him or her. (You can tell him, send her a text, make him a gift, buy her something special, etc.).

As secular parents, we ground our children in the reality of a situation. The above statements represent, as best as we could explain to a young mind, reality. I'm sure you could add to the list. At an age when a child's mind is still open to listening to us, we must repeat these statements and point them out in society whenever possible. For example, we saw a teenage girl who was pregnant at the store one day. Our oldest stared at her for quite a while. When we got to the car, she was full of statements and questions about why the girl was pregnant, how she got that way, and how that will change her life. I relish these conversations because they are real-world examples of the consequences—not just Mom and Dad thinking they know everything.

I once asked some teenagers these questions: What is it that you wanted your parents to tell you about sex that they didn't? Do you talk with your parents about sex? I got one response more than any, especially from boys: "I don't want to talk to my parents about sex at all. Ever." One girl opened up a bit and said she'd be comfortable discussing things like birth control, but, for the most part, teenagers just don't feel like having open conversations about their sexuality. This makes sense. When is the last time you sat down and analyzed your sex life with your parents? Teenagers are young *adults*—and adults for the most part prefer to keep their sexuality between themselves and their partner. Therefore, conversations about sex must happen when children are young because, as teenagers, they close up.

Need another reason to start as young as I am suggesting? How about the latest findings on adolescent and preadolescent girls: Almost fifty percent of African American girls begin their periods by the age of eight. The number is nearly as high for Latin-American girls, and nearly thirty percent of European girls begin at this age as well. Puberty is beginning earlier than it used to. Can you imagine an eight-year-old girl who, though menstruating, doesn't know anything about sex? Think of all the people waiting to take advantage of her ignorance and your failure as a parent?

All this talk about girls doesn't mean boys are immune from these types of discussions. Many adult men will tell you that they thought about sex (though they may not have called it that) nearly all the time as young boys. How do you give boys the moral fortitude to withstand levels of testosterone twice as high as a grown man? First, you let him know that he is not alone. You *talk* with him often and early. My sister is raising my nephew and every time I came to her with "girl problems," she would tell me how she's been working to combat those same issues with her son. My point is that your son needs to know the family's moral stance on sex just as much as your daughters do.

In the end, preparing our children for the world outside our doors is our chief goal, and we can't slack in the area of sex education. It is imperative that we transmit our views on sex in a way that is non-combative and helpful. We can no longer afford to be close-minded on the subject of sex and sexuality; we must broaden our perspective based on the facts that we have. Instead of creating a wall, I'm begging you to inform yourself and your child.

Don't judge; guide. Many parents intending to use the plan outlined above fear that their children will have sex anyway. First, let me say that once your child enters the teen years, they are not your child anymore. They are young adults. You cannot control their behavior, and why would you want to? Young adults need the space to make mistakes. Our goal is not to prevent mistakes; our goal is to make young adults aware of the consequences of their behavior, to offer advice, and to let them know that our love is eternal. Trying to control their behavior will only create a gap in your relationship and result in the young adult's rebellion.

No one *wants* their child to go out and have sex, and, secretly, if I could turn a switch on in my daughters' brains that made sex the most unappealing thing in the world, I would do it. But I can't; no one can.

The time between the ages of thirteen and eighteen is a few precious years when you as the parent must hand over control. You move from parent to guide. You give advice, you let (non-life-threatening) mistakes happen, and you are there to console, teach responsibility, counsel, and refocus when necessary. If you have spent time prepping your child for the decisions that they will have to make, you must trust that they will either make good choices or not, but you can't make any choice for them—no teen will let you!

With this in mind, you must provide a network of people for your child to discuss sex and life with. From a young age, I told my children that if there's something they cannot talk to me about (and there will be those things), call Auntie Courtney or Uncle Jim. Call Grandpa or Grandma Lynn. Call someone who loves them and will give them good advice.

As your children move from elementary school to middle school, deeper conversations about sex and relationships will naturally result. Talk may dissipate during the teen years (except for the occasional "What if?" scenario), as it should. Your young adults are ready to begin making the decisions that will guide their lives— but always with family and friends in the background should they need sound advice.

The Big M: Addressing Masturbation

No chapter in any book about sex is complete without a discussion on masturbation. I'm honestly not sure what all the fuss is about. Actually, that isn't true. There is a lot of fuss surrounding masturbation because it amounts to sheer pleasure for no other reason than that you want to—what my pastor used to call "hedonism." The truth is that masturbation provides relief from strong sexual urges—whether you are an over-stimulated teenage boy or a seasoned thirty-year-old woman. So why is masturbation such a sensitive and guilt-laden topic?

Let's be honest: Masturbation involves a great level of intimacy and privacy. It doesn't make for polite conversation or Facebook updates—and I'm certainly not going to recommend that you sit around the dinner table discussing it. Roughly ninety-five percent of all men and eighty-nine percent of all women admit to masturbating. Here are a few other statistics on masturbation:

- Fewer married Christian men (sixty-one percent) admit to masturbating.

- More than forty percent of males and twenty-two percent of females admit to masturbating daily.

- Studies suggest masturbation may reduce the risk of prostate cancer in men and cervical infections in women.

- At this very moment, roughly 797,151 Americans are masturbating.

If masturbating is so common, where does the guilt come from? Masturbation has been around since man stood up (and probably before), but it became inextricably linked with sin and moral degradation in the early eighteenth century. This occurred when an anonymous writer wrote a publication called *Onania: Or, the Heinous Sin of Self-pollution, and All Its Frightful Consequences (In Both Sexes) Considered.* The book describes masturbation as:

that unnatural practice by which persons of either sex may defile their own bodies, without the assistance of others. Whilst yielding to filthy imagination, they endeavor to imitate and procure for themselves [that which God] has ordered to attend the carnal commerce of the two sexes for the Continuance of our species.

The book would go on to link "self-pollution" with the Genesis story of Onan, a man who spilled his seed upon the ground rather than in the wife of his dead brother and was struck down by God. See any connections between *Onania*'s definition of masturbation and the definition that you were taught as a kid? In my research I came across a woman who wrote that when she was about seven, she was in her room and her mother walked in while she was touching herself. Her mother pulled the covers off her, spent an eternity yelling that she was a dirty girl, and spanked her. To this day, she says the enormous guilt associated with masturbation makes her shower every time she masturbates. She felt so bad about masturbating that, at the age of forty, she locks the door so that her husband won't catch her—and judge her.

Onania went from being a pamphlet to a book as the decades progressed. It was reinforced by religious officials. Even scholars such a Kant and writers like Voltaire acknowledged and promoted the ideas in *Onania*. This practically cemented the view that masturbation was morally corrupt, a belief that was quickly picked up and passed down by parents, enforcing in their children something that was far from the truth.

In reality, masturbation is a normal and healthy part of the human experience. I dare you to find an expert in the field of pediatrics or adolescent medicine that says masturbation is mentally or physically detrimental to a child. In almost every (good) book that deals with sex and children, masturbation is said to be a natural thing that young people shouldn't be made to feel bad about.

Now with all that said, you wouldn't believe how difficult it is to talk with your child about masturbation—at any age. I knew a girl— we'll call her Kim—who would masturbate every day during naptime at the preschool I worked in. My cooperating teacher brought the first incident to my attention. I had no clue what to do. This girl was four years old, sweet as a button, but couldn't keep her hand out of her pants. I didn't want to do or say something that would have an adverse effect on her understanding of sex. I also didn't want the other kids to see her—I just wanted her to stop, really. The idea of a child being aroused on any level was something I just didn't want to think about.

To solve our dilemma, we called our public health nurse. She told us that we should explain to Kim that touching herself in that area was a private matter and should be done in private. We were also told to speak with her parents so that they knew what we told Kim and that it would be good to talk with her about private versus public things. Our public health nurse also gave a presentation on children and masturbation at our next staff development so that there were no misunderstandings. I've been spreading the word ever since.

So now what? Where you go from here when it comes to masturbation depends on a couple things. The first is your child's age. The closer they get to adolescence, the less they will want the word "masturbation" mentioned. They will also have understood the privacy aspect and will most likely avoid public touching. The second is necessity. If your child doesn't bring it up—through their actions or questions—you probably don't need to discuss masturbation.

If the question does arise, or if you notice your child pleasuring themselves, it is a perfect opportunity to explain the difference between public and private things. I do this as casually as possible because, if you seem angry or upset, it may signal to your child that self-pleasure is wrong. I've had to remind children to "please take their hands out of their pants because that's a private thing" before. I say it calmly and I move on. As questions about masturbation come up, answer them honestly and to the point.

If your child is over ten and hasn't talked to you about masturbating, you should assume they've figured it out. Books like *101 Questions about Sex and Sexuality* by Faith Hickman are a good way to give children an opportunity to dive into the subject with dignity and respect—and without you in the room! We put all our books on morality and sex in a general location in our home so that the girls can have access to them at their convenience. No biggie.

As long as you are honest with your child, as long as they can leave a conversation about their bodies with their respect and dignity intact, you will have given them a way to release their sexual energy that carries no risk of STIs, requires no issues of abortion or adoption, and allows them to save sex for later.

10

The Final Frontier:
Death and Other Scary Things

"I was about seven when I really understood

what it meant to die.

Dying meant that my heart would stop.

I wouldn't be able to breathe.

My brain would start to die.

The panic was so real and strong that,

if I think about it long enough,

it will start to creep back into my mind."

It's hard to imagine a time in my life when I won't be able to breathe. Sometimes even the thought of it can make me slightly agitated. I know I'm not alone here. Death is the one realm that we simply can't explore, come back from, and give details. And so, like Einstein sitting on rough patch of grass, most people find that at some point they sit and wonder about the eventuality of death. Is there a heaven? Will I really see loved ones again someday? Does what I do in life even matter?

It is no big surprise that our sense of wonder quickly turns to terror as the questions fall into the black hole that is "life after death." Our fear of the unknown is instinctual and unavoidable. It follows the simple logic of survival: In the wild, fearing the unknown will most certainly save you. Sure, you have to take chances sometimes, but the mantra of "better safe than sorry" has a ton of merit behind it. The big winner, of course, when it comes to human nature and our assumptions about the afterlife is organized religion.

Why? The thought of an afterlife for the devoted, the pure, and the righteous is so perfectly fit for the human mind. Make no mistake: Religion offers an idea of life after death that softly floats our fears about death away. It is the one area where logic *begs* to be made illogical. But we as parents must work to avoid labeling such a temptation as true. We must be willing to confront death openly and honestly. This means facing a fear of death in a new way—uncharted territory. When we talked earlier in the book about critical thinking, we talked about the minds of the very young and their tendency to "cement" the images, ideas, and social norms of parents and close family members. Nowhere is the concept of cementing more evident in our relationship as humans than with death.

We are taught at a critical stage in our mental development, and for the sake of surviving, to fear death. Mostly, this is for good reason: Parents want children to make it to adulthood! *It is necessary that children learn early on in life that they have the power to keep themselves alive.* It is also crucial that children realize death is a part of life; it should not be feared. But getting past our instincts is no easy feat.

Confronting Death Openly and Honestly

The best way to begin such a deep conversation with your child is to start simply: with nature. Secular parents of all stripes recognize that there is a unique relationship between humanity, our world, and the universe. The life-and-death cycle is all around us, yet we do not fear it.

Having discussions with your child about the afterlife also shows the connections that we share with other people and cultures. Our job as parents is to prepare our children for the world that they will inherit. A "twenty-first century child" needs to be able to look past arguments that arise out of faith while at the same time building on the core values that bind us together as human beings, such as shared work toward mutual goals like climate change and the eradication of world hunger.

Sadly, however, religion has caused most children to enter their adult lives with a focus on "their God," the purpose *he* has for them, and how to deal with those who commit treason against the "Almighty." This isn't a bashing session here. I see religion as a natural phenomenon of the human mind. But religion, like all other phenomena, is not without fault. Whether on purpose or by default, religion teaches the young mind that the afterlife is a reward for devotion to the faith.

Teaching children a perception of life after death that strips religion of its power is absolutely necessary and overdue. I had a professor in college who tried. Every day when we walked into biology class, he would stare at us for a long time and then announce in a calm and normal voice, "All of you are going to die. One day, each and every one of you will stop breathing and die." After that he'd go on teaching class like he'd said nothing—every single day of the semester. I knew then what he was trying to do, and I knew it was hard to think about it. It was easier to just call him the crazy bio teacher. What was he trying to tell us (besides the obvious)? Why did he think we didn't know?

Really, conversations about death should begin long before a quirky professor decides to share his thoughts on the subject. Many children are not afforded such an offer. Death is couched in fear, pain, and at times complete confusion. Often, we only talk about death when someone dies, at which point sadness looms over the conversation, forever shaping a child's view of the afterlife. Our society has a habit of shielding young people in the hopes of keeping them forever pure. When it comes to discussions of death, we do a huge disservice to them. Instead of allowing our children to have a relationship with death that is based on fear, we must teach them to understand what death is and why it is so important to life. Conversations about death and dying should come with a regularity that promotes understanding and offers support in times of need.

But how does one actually go about such a conversation? One day you and I will die. While coming to terms with our mortality becomes easier the longer we live, it is the youngest of us who deserve a way of understanding death that simultaneously allows them to enjoy life. Our family experienced such a need when our girls were very young, just three and four years old. My nephew was diagnosed with pediatric neuroblastoma, a particularly aggressive cancer that presented itself when he himself was barely two. He would not live long past his third birthday.

As a secular parent—and a mother and aunt—I was presented with challenges on more than one level: how to discuss a fatal illness, how to move from illness to death, and how to discuss and move through the grieving process with myself and my children. My goal is to share with you some of the techniques for opening a dialogue on a discussion about death and dying. This isn't all-inclusive. As usual with secular parenting, it will be through further reading that you gain a wide perspective on the subject.

I scoured the internet (which was still rather new to me at that time) for ways to talk about death with children. It was important for me to keep honesty and truth at the forefront of such a delicate conversation. All the information I found online referred to "a better place" after death, but it was exactly that kind of conversation that I wanted to avoid.

We'd had no religious faith at the time and I'd decided that I wasn't going to "find religion" for this occasion either. What was more frustrating was that we had not had a death in the family during my daughters' lifetimes; this would be their first experience with death. The first of anything sets the tone for future patterns. After talking with my husband, we decided to be very honest with the girls. The truth of the matter is that we only knew what physically happens to a person when they die—and so that was what we worked hard to explain.

First, we explained. We told the girls that their cousin had cancer. It took some questioning because, as predicted, neither knew what cancer was. So what did we do? We grabbed paper and some crayons and we drew pictures. What did we draw? We drew the human cell. Since I'm not artist, our cell lacked everything but a nucleus. We talked about what a healthy cell is and what happens when a cell has cancer. My oldest said that that would "hurt your body if it happened too much" and that let me know that we needed to move on to the next part of the conversation.

Next, we explained more. This time the focus was on the diagnosis, and what it means for something or someone who was alive to die. This was hard. After a while, I didn't fight the tears. Sadness is a part of loss. As long as a person doesn't stay there, trapped in sadness, I see no problem with sharing those emotions with a child. How nice it is to know that you aren't the only one feeling that way. Once the children realized that the doctors weren't going to be able to fix cancer, my oldest asked us if she too was going to die. We said that her body would get tired of trying to fix itself and it would stop working. This was by far the hardest part of our conversation, but pushing through our sadness to get to the question was invaluable.

We asked *them* about death. I wanted to know what their thoughts on death were. Sure, they were young. (My youngest was barely focused on our conversation. We figured this would happen, but she deserved to be there.) I just threw it out there: "Girls, *what do you think about death?*" Before I gave them any of my views, I wanted to know what came to mind when they thought of death. Mostly they talked about not being able to breathe and how it would make them sad. I let them speak until they were finished with all of their thoughts.

Instead of putting the religious conversation first ("You know, girls, some people believe . . ."), we focused instead on their cousin. They had been to hospital to see him a couple times. They said that people go to the hospital to get fixed when they are hurt. We talked about how it hurts to have something wrong with your body. Cancer is painful. There are needles and medicine that makes you sick. Cancer makes your body hurt. Their young cousin could not leave the hospital, go to school, or even be around most people. He could not be near flowers, ants, or pools. He was unhappy.

We found backup. First, we told them the only fact that we know about death: When you die, you do not feel any pain. We talked about how it would be sad when their cousin's body stopped working. There would be a funeral and they would not attend. And even though we would be sad about him dying, even though we would miss him very much, he wouldn't be in pain anymore and that was a good thing. We also had pamphlets that children can read about death and a few books that my sister had about confronting death. These are excellent resources that a hospital or community clinic would be more than happy to provide.

It was through the pamphlets (and later conversations) that the girls became very curious. They wanted to know the process of dying ("Does it hurt when a body is about to stop working?"). They also wondered how we knew the things that we were saying. Did a doctor tell us?

Finally, we discussed the emotions associated with death. We all cope with our mortality differently. The similarity lies in those stages of grief that we *all* inevitably travel through: denial (or isolation), anger, bargaining, depression, and acceptance.[21] I wanted our children's first conversations about death to be in a calm and safe manner, not jagged and confusing like my own childhood experiences. I also needed them to internalize some truisms that don't take the pain away but do add a level of understanding to the flood of emotions that come with loss. We told the children:

- Everyone dies. Your body cannot live forever and *that is OK*. Plants die, animals and bugs die, and humans die.

- When you die, you are not in pain because your brain cannot feel pain anymore.

- When someone dies, we can use pictures to remember them, we can write or talk about them, and we can always think about them.

- Life is precious. We are lucky to breathe air and so we must take care of our minds and our bodies until they are done working.

---

[21]I would encourage you to seek out information on the stages of grief either online or in print form. Internalizing this information will help you and your child(ren) through the passing of a loved one.

- Since death is a part of life, there is no fear in talking about it at any time. Whenever you feel like you want to have a conversation with me about this, I'll listen to you.

The conversation we had with our children was limited to their age (three and four). For you and your child, discussing the death of a loved one will not be exactly the same. You may have a teenager who is having trouble dealing with loss. You may have a smaller child who is throwing a tantrum because they want to go to Grandma's and they have no idea what death, dying, or any of that other "adult" vocabulary means. *The sooner you begin a dialogue on death as a part of life, the sooner you will cement associations that take the fear out of death.* The best way to do this is with honesty.

What about the religious question? My children never brought it up. I would have told them my views on God, heaven, and hell. I would also have told them that not everyone looks at things the way I do. I would have explained to them that, when they are older and they've had lots of years to think about things, they can decide what is best for them to believe. I wouldn't end the conversation without saying our family motto: *I will love you no matter what you choose.* It didn't happen overnight, but death is no longer a scary subject in our home. Sometimes we pull out little Khabir's pictures. My daughters see him smiling, talk about his personality, and sometimes they cry.

The next time that our family experienced a loss, my children responded quite differently. We lost their beloved Aunt Rebecca when the girls were seven and eight years old. The chain of events and their responses, particularly my oldest daughter's, would add another layer to the conversation about the afterlife that we had.

Rebecca had been a part of the girl's life since we'd moved to Missouri when they were small children. She was an aunt you could only dream up: smart, funny, and full of goodness. Any problem they had, Rebecca had a positive solution. So when she decided to solve her own problems by swallowing a concoction of prescription pills, it threw everyone off balance.

We arrived at Rebecca's house in the middle of the night, an ambulance greeting us. My daughters' cousin was still asleep, the girls themselves were plopped on the couch with blankets, and my husband and I were trying to get as much information as possible. We would learn that summer the power of memory. We would follow the same steps of conversation. We explained what suicide was, we talked about what it meant to be in a vegetative state, and we talked about losing Rebecca.

One major consideration before having conversations about the afterlife with children is how you personally feel about death, loss, and possibilities beyond life. As a child, death was a scary thing for me. I'd been to funerals and even been made to touch and kiss the bodies of lost loved ones. I didn't want to. I had horrible nightmares after funerals and I'd vowed to never attend them as an adult. Essentially, I'd blocked off the emotions needed to engage a child (or any person, for that matter) about how it feels to lose a loved one— and how to move on in a healthy way. But this presents a real problem for parents. Our children need us to move through the process of loss if they are to emerge emotionally and socially well.

That was evident to me when we were driving down the street one day about six months after Rebecca's suicide when my daughter unexpectedly burst into tears. I had no idea that death was on her mind. We were on the freeway and a loud ambulance passed us. As I looked over my shoulder to merge back into traffic, I discovered my daughter in tears.

"What's wrong?" I asked.

"The sirens reminded me of Auntie Becca," she replied.

The sirens reminded me of Auntie Becca.

That was the farthest thing from my mind. All I could do, the only semblance of emotion I could muster, was to say that I was sorry. I turned the music up and tried to disappear as we drove home.

But that wasn't good enough. My daughter deserved to have those emotions at the least acknowledged and worked through. Since the stages of grief revolve and cycle, I wanted my approach to discussing death to do the same. Later that day, I grabbed the photo album, made some hot chocolate, and looked through it with both girls. When we came to a picture of Rebecca, we talked about those stages and where we might be in our feelings (we were in different places). I also reiterated things that we could do to help us move forward—like looking through photos and journaling our feelings.

For some of us, the amount of conversation necessary can seem overwhelming, or even unnecessary. The key is short, focused dialogue with your child. You know them better than anyone. Without a patient parent, one who is willing to devote small moments of clear conversation, a child may be left with guilt, anguish, and confusion.

Not only have we discussed death in detail with our children— and the sadness and joys that can come from remembrance—we've also discussed our wishes when we die. As your child ages, these types of conversations will inevitably happen. My children know that when I die I would like to have my body donated to science. I have no desire for them or anyone else to see my body in an open casket—only making their last memory of me more disturbed than it needs to be.

Why would I tell my children such things? Why *not?* One day I *will* die and hopefully they will still be alive. These conversations aren't morbid or overly lengthy; typically they spring up off-the-cuff.

Contrary to what some might think, we do not have depressed or anxious children as a result.

Should your children become overly anxious or preoccupied with death, open communication is the key to helping them work through their anxiety. Don't feel you and your partner can handle the job? Find some trusted family and friends who share your opinions on death, read books on helping children cope with death, or seek counseling. The point is to have a child who grows into an adult whose mindset on the afterlife is stable, well-informed, and as balanced as possible.

"A fearful child is an obedient child.
And we all want obedient children, right?"

Of course not everyone would want to see children work through their fears about death. For a great many in America, a fearful child *is* an obedient child: nothing less will suffice. In making decisions about how to help your child have a positive relationship with death, I would encourage parents to also take a hard look at those things which perpetuate the very fear that we are working to neutralize.

The best place to begin is with media, mostly because it touches us in so many ways. To ignore its presence would be foolish. Our family's relationship to media is a sense of fusion that's easy to sum up: we are a house of "techies." My children have always had (guarded) access to the internet. Our music and movie collection is on par with the average American—if the average American's music and movie collection was doubled. Every bedroom and office in our house has at least three or four large posters, and our girls can navigate flash drives, external hard drives, AVI (Audio Video Interleave) files, and media tanks like most children use Legos.

When it comes to actual movies, I was raised in the heyday of horror films. Fear of an "afterlife" first came to me in that form— and for many children, it still does today. Watching horror films as young children instills fear at a time when ideas are cemented into the brain, making them so much more than "scary movies." By the time I was ten, and thanks to unsupervised access to HBO, Cinemax, and the other giants of television, I'd seen enough horror films to last a lifetime. As an adult, they are awesome relics of movie magic, but as a child, I was warped by the possibilities they showed me. I was far too young to see movies that depicted violent murders, sadists, demon children, and torture devices.

For each of us, scary movies have their place. For some, movies like *Night of the Living Dead* are a great watch. For others, at the first change in music we hide our eyes, making the movie more heard than seen. Unfortunately, many children are exposed to movies that instill fear at extremely young and impressionable ages. I have no idea how, but I'm sure that I'd seen every scary movie the sixties, seventies, and eighties produced before I was twelve years old. No one forced me to watch them. I was just a young kid who didn't want to go to bed and had unfettered access to TV channels at all hours of the night. I'd stay awake on weekends for hours afraid of Freddy, Jason, Jaws or some other horrid creature.

What I am not saying is that these movies are evil and should never be watched. What I am saying is that these movies create a sense of fear and wonder that is healthy—if you understand that it's a movie. Some of the more recent movies to hit the theatres like the Saw series are so psychologically terrifying that I'd classify them as harmful if watched at young ages—in other words, exactly what we are trying to avoid.

I caution against children, even those as old as nine, watching such horrible things. They are fun for some of us; we know these movies are movies and we enjoy the adrenaline rush! Children, on the other hand, are still creating their understanding of the world and these movies have the potential to create associations—especially without some sort of debriefing about what they have seen—that are wholly negative and can last for a lifetime. If you add those movies with religious overtones, you get a match designed to promote conformity to faith through fear—but more on that in minute.

We also don't want to desensitize our children to the pain and suffering of others. We want our children to grow up recognizing the neglected people of the world. We want young children that see a child being bullied and step in. We want children of moral strength and integrity, not children who could care less about the pain of their fellow human beings.

Make no mistake: I am not angry with the movie industry. It is their job to find creative ways to tap into the emotion of their viewers and make money. I'm actually saying that they do their job well. For the very young, fear, audio-visuals, and religious overtones can create dangerously toxic mental ideas. Sadly, there is a growing trend in America and throughout the world to do just that. As parents we must balance being "overprotective" and denying all fun when it comes to fear and the afterlife with conversations that make such distinctions very clear.

Returning to the idea of using fear to keep children in line, there is another more sinister way to corrupt a healthy relationship with the afterlife. These are called Hell Houses. A Hell House is one of the most sick and twisted things religious organizations use to trick a child into believing the religious version of an afterlife—and they're becoming a staple in many communities.

Mirrored in the image of traditional haunted houses, Hell and Judgment Houses are designed to "scare people into loving Christ" by graphically depicting those things that God does not like. Glenn Beck spoke about Hell Houses in 2006. He said, "You know what I feel like? I feel like one of those 'Yes, but' Muslims that I always talk about when it comes to terrorism. Yes, I disagree with what they've done, but I understand what they're doing. It's the same thing here." Glenn goes on to chastise the pastor he was speaking to, but chastising and being fervently against are not the same. To endorse—either overtly or covertly—this type of psychological torture is sick.

I should note that many Christians are against the idea of Hell Houses. But somehow, their voices are overlooked in the religious community:

The Colorado Council of Churches criticized the scare tactics used in the Arvada Hell House in that state.

Reverend J.T. Tucker, director of youth ministries at Northway Christian Church in Dallas, Texas, commented that "trying to scare people into a decision [for Jesus] is very wrong . . . If you consider all the money, along with ministry hours . . . if they would refocus those areas on missions in urban Dallas, I think they would have a lot bigger return . . ."

Reverend Ballard's Hell House in Warren County, Ohio, was criticized by Doreen Cudnik, executive director of Stonewall Cincinnati. She said that "to say gay equals AIDS equals burning in hell has the dangerous potential to lead to hate crimes against the gay community."[22]

What's worse, many of the scenes in Hell Houses are purposefully skewed. For example many Hell Houses feature a scene on abortion. What they generally show is a near-full term baby being aborted—heads are ripped off, arms and legs torn apart. The fact is that only about one percent of abortions in America occur *after* the first trimester. Yet what is cemented is the image of innocent children near birth being mutilated and murdered.

The frustration that any parent should have with using fear as a way to gain compliance is that ultimately it does not work. There are times, especially as my daughters have begun maturing into young women, when I've wanted a magic wand to make them do what I say. What parent doesn't? But if our goal is creating people who can think for themselves and make good decisions on their own, fear is not the answer to our frustrations as parents.

The answer, of course, is education. Remember: You cannot stop teenagers from doing what they want to do. Parents who try end up in power struggles that tend to end in an ugly manner. What you *can* do is tell them how you feel, outline the consequences for actions

---

[22]Information taken from http://www.religioustolerance.org/hallo_he.htm.

(positive and negative), and keep the lines of communication open. That's parenting at the young adult level: not control but knowledge, facts, love, and support. There's no excuse to justify the mental torture of children because they don't always listen to God's rules.

The scariest part of a Hell House "tour" comes at the end. You are put in a room with two doors, the one you came through and a mystery door. A pastor stands in front of you and says that if you didn't like what you saw, there is a person behind the door who can help you avoid hell. They are not told that there are people who live wonderful lives without Christ. They are not told that hell, heaven, and God are all subjects that are regularly debated on an academic and social level. No, they are told that these things are facts and that they risk their mortal soul by not walking through the door. It's pathetic.

The only reason that authorities, and people like Mr. Beck, have not cracked down on the exploitation of children in a case such as this can be spelled using only three little letters: God. Each Hell House skit is equal to a mini snuff movie where any sane, critically-thinking person is enraged before the end of the first minute. But since we are not allowed to address the absurd rituals in any religion in an objective way, officials (and religious parents) look the other way. Fear can teach nothing more than an instinct not to die. If you want your children to make long-lasting positive choices, they need to understand the past, present, and future consequences of their actions.

Instead of spending thousands and making thousands mentally abusing children, churches can set up trusts funds to help abused children in our country, funnel more money into youth in poverty programs, and generate funds to help children who live under the poverty line. These types of things help young children see the kindness of religious individuals, not how sick and warped their mind is in the name of God.

To help your child have a healthier point of view about the dangers that children can encounter in the world, I suggest the documentary route. We watched a documentary called *Shocking! The World's Smallest People* as a family. It showed the lives of families with dangerously small children in America and Canada. The documentary led us to conversations on genetics, nature, overcoming tough challenges, and liking oneself. These qualities were seen through the stories of real people. We went online and learned about foundations to which the girls wanted to send some of their allowance money. You can teach your children to be responsible adults with love and compassion—not fear and submission.

A Hands-On Approach

A final aspect of death and dying that is worth noting is the idea of giving children an active role in the ritual of death. Ritual? Yes. For some families—both secular and non-secular—having children actively participate in the death process—the caring for and the preparation of the body—is a way to say goodbye to loved ones and begin the mourning process. This is a personal decision that really revolves around family dynamics, the age of the children, and your personal idea of what it would take to bring closure to your family. I first came across an article by Joy Johnson on this subject and found it quite fascinating. I'd always assumed that complete separation— until an age that warranted further connection with death—was appropriate. It is true that, for many children, our current rituals tend to create confusion and unnecessary feelings of fear. For example, when my stepfather died I was made to touch and kiss his body even though I was screaming and crying. However, it is also true that being part of the process of death—acknowledging the loss of life in a tangible way—can have a therapeutic effect that aids the process of grief. There are a few ways to accomplish this.

Use cherished items. One way to move a child through the loss of a parent, a loved one, or even a pet is to identify cherished items that become a sort of offering to those who have left our presence. In Joy Johnson's article on children and funerals, she offers us a nugget of truth. She says that "Americans are just now beginning to see the value of involving children in funeral planning and participation when a loved one dies." Her article opens by offering examples of children contributing to the funeral process with items that would be of value to the one lost: "boots . . . a favorite coffee cup . . . M&Ms." These items, while trivial on the outside, provide a tangible sense of closure for children.

Let children understand the process. In addition to Joy's suggestions, you may have children who have grown desensitized and want to know the exact processes involved in preparing the body for burial. I have not had such a conflicting conversation with my children. If any parent is in such a situation, I can only hope they recognize this reality: Everyone deals with death in different ways. I would caution a parent against looking at a child's inquiry into the processes of cremation, embalming, and (in particularly tragic and violent losses of life) the "fixing" of a body as gross, bad, or otherwise negative. Remember that children are curious. Understanding what is happening offers a sense of security.

Allow the child to decide whether to attend the funeral. Above all, I stress that in something as sensitive a matter as this, a child should have a choice to attend or remain separate from the funeral services. As a rule, I believe that children under five should not attend funeral services; it makes the last image of a parent or loved one forever attached to death. There are ways to help young people grieve in a way that leaves the most salient images of loved ones—playing card games, giving hugs, or snuggling on the couch—the strongest in a small child's mind. If you are going to give a child that young the option of going to a funeral, it is very important that they be as prepared as possible. They should know that this is a quiet, focused space; that they will see their loved one, but that this loved one will not respond; that they will move to another place to bury the body, etc. Information and patience will help the day run as smoothly as possible under the circumstances.

Home Burial: Connecting at the Surface Level

While the majority of us will leave this world via cremation, funeral, and ceremony, a movement toward home burial is underway. The overwhelming amount of strength it would take to bury a loved one myself—or yourself—seems unfathomable, yet hundreds of families decide to undertake such a challenge each year. It begins at a level of intimacy with death that few Americans are akin to. Lisa Carlson began writing books on the subject twenty-five years ago. In an article she wrote for the *Huffington Post*, Jaweed Kaleem asked Carslon to recount the negativity she experienced. "I was pretty much treated as a freak," Carlson explained. "Today, twenty-five years later, I get an inquiry every day, or almost every day [asking about home burials]." I found Carlson, her book, and the entire subject of home burial fascinating. What are the rules to such a personal approach with death? Would such an experience help shape, in a fundamentally positive way, the relationship that children have with death?

As with every aspect of parenting, I found out that there are no rules. Families choose to do a home burial for several reasons, and children are involved at varying levels. Of late, several organizations have begun reaching out to families across the country who want to say goodbye to loved ones on their own terms. Kaleem's article lists a few, such as "Crossings, a Maryland-based home funeral resource organization," the National Home Funeral Alliance, and Final Passages. The list goes on, and each year more community-based organizations are created. Barring a few considerations, I think this is a welcome trend that many communities throughout the world experience as a part of daily life.

Discuss end of life issues with children *before* loss of life. Whether your desire is to be cremated, placed in a traditional casket, or given a home funeral, it is important to have multiple conversations on the subject of how you would like to be treated after death. In the case of a home or intimate burial, it is even more important for children to be able to ask questions and voice concerns that may put them at ease when your life ends. The fewer surprises, the easier it will be for your child to go through the grieving process.

Discuss the actual process. In the case of home burials, and in instances of prolonged illnesses, children should be aware of the fact that a body changes color and will need ice and other necessities after death. As with all things, parents, you know your child better than anyone. This means that you know how far to go, what to cover in depth, and the need to ask "probing questions" such as, *What part of this sounds a little confusing?* Or, *let's take a break and talk more about this later, OK?* In cases where a parent or loved one has been dealing with illness for quite some time, where death is an eventuality, it may be prudent to have someone else work with children as they process. In any case, small nuggets of information are always preferable to long sermons.

Always give children an "opt-out" card. It is easy for us as parents to say "this is what our family is going to do" and move past without considering a child's desires. This would be a failure on our part. We know from experience that being told "you must" when it comes to decisions that really should be a matter of choice can have negative consequences. Yes, it may be very important—from your family's standpoint—to have children participate in the cleaning and final rites of a loved one, but to what extent can a child refuse? Consider that there are many ways a child can move through the grieving process without the handling of a loved one's body. Finding catharsis is a personal path. Don't force your method on your children—their path may be different.

I was intrigued by the home burial prospect, and my husband and I discussed it at length when I began reading articles on the subject. I concluded that it was something I wasn't comfortable with, something that mentally I didn't believe I could handle. He agreed, and you may agree as well. If, however, you find this aspect of end-of-life care palatable for your family, I would certainly suggest doing research and beginning conversations in your home on the subject.

Whether you choose home burial, traditional burial, or something in between, conversations with your child on the subject as they reach an age where such a topic seems appropriate will only broaden their perspective on a subject that has been shrouded in unnecessary mystery and confusion.

The Journey, The Now, and The Future

The journey of writing this book has been one full of self-doubt: what if in the end, no one reads it? What if no one likes it? In many ways this book—this unique idea of secular parenting—is my baby. I have watched it break, fall down a few times, and finally it has emerged—stronger for the weather. Presenting it to the world is no easy feat. Like our children, it needed constant molding and redirecting for a world that may not love it as much as myself. The plan fell into place the way many sometimes do: accidentally. But as I look back, a clear process rose from the chaos of the last 10 years.

The first step on that journey of course was to move past my anger. It was beyond frustrating to have people branding your child before they've even had the chance to prove their merit. At the same time, that mama bear approach of slashing everyone to bits wouldn't ease my anger (though, sometimes in my mind that would seem just). In all seriousness, however, learning to move past anger in a healthy way will help both you and your children learn the art of perseverance in god-fearing world.

Writing was a way for me to do two things as a mother: quell the frustration that gave way to anger many times, and offer a sense of hope and inspiration for those parents who have to go through their own secular parenting "trial by fire". Between scribbling notes for the book and pouring my heart out on the blog, I began to feel lighter. Motivated even. If you are in a situation similar to the one I found myself in, the first step is to find a healthy outlet for the waves for sadness and frustration that will surly test your reserves.

After my first draft was finished, it was placed where most English teachers place their first book: on a shelf. I'd made my copy, said my peace, and in general felt better. But just as we must revisit thoughts and ideas with our children, I knew my book—my baby— would need revisiting before I could present her. It would take two major revisions over the course of 5 years—in between finishing a Master's degree, becoming an educator, and an ultimatum to myself—before I found an agent, an editor, and got serious about charting a vision for parenting that a secular parent could appreciate.

The process reminded me that we as parents have a drive that we must all tap into: this world will try at every turn to steer our children down a path that they have pre-chosen. Whether it be in the realm of religion, politics, and especially, morality is of no consequence, we must take that power from a confused society. Being the guiding force in our children's lives AND allowing them the opportunity to choose their path as a unique individual is the ultimate answer. It has no direct road of travel. I worked hard to find all the avenues of possibility that I could muster, but you will undoubtedly chart a path that doesn't follow the same line that I've experienced.

My vision for secular parenting is long and wide. Whether it is called secular parenting, parenting with child choice in mind, or anything in between, my promise is to spend my life promoting it. It is not to the detriment of faith that I do this. My frustration has never been with the fact that faith exists, my frustration lies only with the predominance of faith as a guiding principal for parenting. Our children deserve the full range of philosophical understanding, and we can give them that because they deserve to know *all* they can while they move through this world.

Parenting in this way has been a joy, an absolute thrill! I can't tell you how many times I've looked at my girls and thought, did they really just teach me that? I can even say that there have been *plenty* of arguments that I have lost because my children approached my illogical stance with critical thinking. Those are times we wished our children new less!

But that is only the pride of adulthood talking. Having a child challenge the logic upon which your argument is built, respectfully and sincerely, should be an expectation of *all* parents. It is that kind of critical thinking that really does help them as they go into a world that tries at every turn to diminish those same skills.

From here my journey moves into the secular community itself. I'd like to explore how we, as a microcosm, relate to one another. My questions are broad: how does being secular in the Midwest differ from being secular in the northeast? What role does race, gender, and sexual orientation play in how we as a community interact? Do we interact at all? I'm sure all of these questions can be answered with books of their own, and though I won't promise to write them, I will promise to keep doing what *all* secular parents must: I will keep learning.

Acknowledgements

My heartfelt thanks to:

Dr. David Partenheimer. Thank you for giving me honest feedback, and thank you for always supporting my dream of becoming a writer. Thank you for editing chapters, and refocusing my passion when it went down a dark path. Truman State is fortunate to have you and I feel lucky to have stumbled upon your mythology class all those years ago.

Keilah Sullivan, for being a rock-star editor. You, young lady, are poised for great things. I feel so privileged to have met you when I did. Thank you for keeping me on track, and thank you for being authentic with your thoughts. Your honesty kept me balanced as a writer.

My sister Sakara Remmu, for being my personal cheerleader in parenting. From loading our collective six children into a movie theatre, to letting me vent over the insanity of teenage angst, you have been my "parent therapist" for nearly fifteen years now. I love you dearly, and I wouldn't be the parent I am today without you.

My girls, Essie, AJ, and Rah—mostly for those very first lies; they started this book rolling! You girls are an inspiration to me: smart, beautiful, and completely hilarious. I feel so lucky to be your mom, and I can't wait to see all the cool adventures that each of you will have as you sail through life.

Josh, for enduring scribbles on the Buddha statue, rocks as car-cleaning agents, teary-eyed, high-pitch screaming girls, and all other things dad. Thank you for being my partner in parenting and the love of my life. This book wouldn't exist without you, and our girls wouldn't be who they are without their Joshie. Thank you for reading chapters, suggesting books, and gluing me back together when I fall apart.

About the Author

Be-Asia McKerracher was born and raised in Seattle, WA. She moved to the Midwest in 2003 to begin her career as an educator at Truman State University. Be-Asia is also known as **The Secular Parent** online. Her website (secularparent.com), which began in 2006, was originally a way to deal with the frustrations of being a nonreligious parent in the Midwest. Now, it has become a place of respite for secular parents in America and around the world.

In 2008 Be-Asia participated in The Kansas City Star's *Faith Walk* series, publishing four articles on the topic of children and faith. As a result of her work with The Kansas City Star British-based publication *The Freethinker* invited Mrs. McKerracher to publish a longer, in-depth article on the subject of children and faith. Her article, *Challenging the Myth: An Expose of the 'Divinity' of the Young Child*, was published in 2009.

Be-Asia earned her B.A. and Master's degrees through Truman State University in English in 2006 and 2009, respectively. In 2010, she became an adjunct faculty member with University of Missouri's High School/College Partnerships program (HSCP). She currently lives in Kansas City, MO, with her husband and two teenage children.